Greenhill Books

THEY FELL LIKE STONES

Ah! those red soldiers at Isandlwana,
How few they were, and how they fought!
They fell like stones – each man in his place.

– A Zulu Warrior

'IN MEMORIAM' – THEY FELL LIKE STONES

THEY FELL LIKE STONES

BATTLES AND CASUALTIES
OF THE ZULU WAR, 1879

by John Young

With a new Introduction
by Kenneth Griffith

Greenhill Books, London
Presidio Press, California

This edition of *They Fell Like Stones*
first published 1991 by Greenhill Books, Lionel Leventhal Limited,
Park House, 1 Russell Gardens, London NW11 9NN
and
Presidio Press, P.O. Box 1764, Novato, Ca.94948, U.S.A.

British Library Cataloguing in Publication Data
Young, John
They fell like stones : battles and casualties of the Zulu War, 1879.
I. Title
968.4045

ISBN 1-85367-096-0

Library of Congress Cataloging-in-Publication Data
Young, John.
They fell like stones : battles and casualties of the Zulu War, 1879 /
by John Young; with a new introduction by Kenneth Griffith.
p. cm.
Includes bibliographical references and index.
ISBN 1-85367-096-0
1. Zulu War. 1879—Campaigns.   2. Zulu War. 1879—Casualties
(Statistics, etc.)   3. Zulu War. 1879—Registers of dead.
I. Title
DT1875.Y68   1991
968.4'045—dc20   91-23564
CIP

Photoset by Rowland Phototypesetting Limited,
Bury St Edmunds, Suffolk
Printed in Great Britain by Biddles Limited, Guildford, Surrey

Contents

Introduction

by Kenneth Griffith

I N ALL of my life I have never known a person so conversant, in such minute detail, with any subject, as John Young is with the Anglo-Zulu War of 1879. And what is more, his knowledge laps alarmingly into other British military areas. My own subject is the Second British-Boer War of 1899 to 1902, and when speaking about it in John's presence I have to voice my 'facts' *very* carefully because if I am a little off the mark I will hear a significant clearing of the throat or some other sign of discomfiture. I also know that in making this categorical statement about John's supremacy in knowledge of that unforgivable war I have made mild enemies of every other 'Zulu War' enthusiast in Britain at least (and in Britain, it seems to me, you can't move for Zulu enthusiasts; they are everywhere). Great enthusiasts, in any subject, *have* to believe that they are the best; actors and actresses are similar; if they stop suspecting that they are the very best they are in danger of sinking into oblivion.

Which leads me to academics. I have never asked John what his 'qualifications' might be; that is printed ones, issued by a university. I suspect none; he has been too busy acting positively (*too* positively some might say!) as a police constable. But as a very careful betting man I would put every penny I possess on John as against any learned gentleman at Oxford or Cambridge on the subject in question. What losses our educational system suffers by barring all of us who truly *know*, simply because we haven't won the required academic degrees!

And John's knowledge does not stop at hard facts; it extends perceptively into the psychology of the soldiers (Zulu and British) and of the politicians involved. John's perception of history is bursting at the seams to escape and communicate itself.

We have become mutual friends because I once made a film for the British Broadcasting Corporation commemorating the centenary of this Anglo-Zulu War. I titled it *Black as Hell: Thick as Grass*. In John Young's mind it passes muster. A great compliment. And we have become such loyal chums that when a distinguished British officer is mentioned in the film and another officer's face appears to represent him, John refrains from audibly groaning (in my defence I was out of Britain working on some other project when these 'graphics' were selected).

I have had the privilege of wandering over the ghost-ridden area of Isandlwana and Rorke's Drift, etc. on different occasions: John has never seen Zululand. This must be rectified.

One last point. John has refrained from being subjective in this book. He has confined his writings to the hardest of facts. I want to see his next work push out into his invaluable opinions.

KENNETH GRIFFITH

Preface

'WHERE IS the Englishman who does not regard the war with Cetywayo [sic] and his Zulus with mingled feelings? Is it likely that interest in the campaign will ever fade? Surely not.' Words not written recently but in the 1880s by W. Pimblett in his book *In Africa with the Union Jack*. Clearly the interest has held. I embarked on this project of researching the casualties of the war only after a lengthy interest in the subject.

I first became interested in the Anglo-Zulu War of 1879 when, at a tender age, I was taken by my father, William, to see the film *Zulu*. My father embellished the tale by recalling the Regimental history lessons he had attended whilst serving with the Monmouthshire Regiment, one of the Territorial battalions of the South Wales Borderers. The SWBs were formed under the Cardwell reforms of 1881, having previously been designated the 24th (2nd Warwickshire) Regiment of Foot, whose deeds are synonymous with the Anglo-Zulu War. The only reading material I could find then on the subject was my brother's copy of *The Wonder Book of Daring Deeds* which contained a brief chapter on Rorke's Drift.

My enthusiasm grew and in 1978 I joined the Victorian Military Society, a happy band of enthusiasts interested in the wars of colonial expansion of the nineteenth century. My research became an obsession – a lust for more knowledge. I can still recall rushing home to see a television documentary on 22nd January 1979, one hundred years on from the two differing battles of the campaign, Isandlwana and Rorke's Drift. The documentary was Kenneth Griffith's *Black as Hell, Thick as Grass*. Little did I know that the fine Welsh character actor who, in the documentary, conveyed such roles as diverse as the aloofness of Sir Henry Bartle Edward Frere and the

9

Cockney resolve of Private Fred Hitch, VC, with such ease, would, in the fullness of time, become such a friend. I must express my extreme thanks to Kenneth, for the great assistance he has given me in the compilation of this book, for his kind words in the introduction, and for his friendship.

George Rice, photographer and artist, has also been a source of encouragement. When I had sustained a serious injury which delayed the completion of this book, it was George's words of advice that caused me to persevere with the project. Without George's assistance this book would also lack any illustrations. I am deeply indebted to him.

My thanks also go to others: Keith Reeves for his help; David Whybrow and Jack Webb for their joint knowledge on the details of the 57th Regiment of Foot – The Middlesex Regiment; Gordon Everson on allowing me to tap his knowledge on the Isandlwana casualties and the Rorke's Drift defenders; to Mark Coghlan for his assistance on the Natal Carbineers, and I take this opportunity to express my regret in having been so tardy in my correspondence. I hope this 'public' apology is acceptable. The staffs of the Public Record Office and National Army Museum for their help in providing the resources at their disposal. The ladies of my local branch of the Essex County Library Service, for procuring certain books through the inter-library loan scheme. To Major R.P. Smith and his staff at the South Wales Borderers and Monmouthshire Museum for allowing me on my last visit to Brecon to delve into the records of the 'Glorious 24th'. The Regimental Secretary of the Staffordshire Regiment, for positively identifying one of their Isandlwana survivors. David Parry, curator of the Rhodes Birthplace Museum, for placing at my disposal the records appertaining to the Zulu War held there. For those I have encountered along the way, some of whom I have lost contact with: Ian Knight, Terry Lyons, George Smith, Patricia D'Arcy, Martin Boswell, Graham Faulkner, John Poyner, John Lester, Geoff Robertson and Dennis Slack, all of whom in some way have added to my knowledge and understanding of the Anglo-Zulu War of 1879.

I do not say that my work is without fault, but I hope any errors I have made are minor. I have not attempted to resolve the enigma of Isandlwana. I have left that to others. I have included in the casualties of the Siege of Eshowe those who succumbed to their illnesses and disease whilst awaiting their relief since I consider that those men were the subject of a military action – siege. I have excluded casualties sustained by what the American forces refer to as 'friendly fire', the accidental killing or wounding of forces by their own arms except when it occurred in battle.

There is one person without whose assistance this work would not have come to fruition – my wife Lorraine. Apart from coping as a wife and mother to our two young children, Toby and Nicholas, she has meticulously typed and corrected this work. She has tolerated my interest for long dead men and for a far-away place I have yet to see: Zululand.

JOHN YOUNG

THE ILLUSTRATIONS

With a few exceptions, the illustrations in this book are from two rival illustrated newspapers available in Great Britain at the time of the Anglo-Zulu War of 1879. *The Graphic* and *The Illustrated London News* were the 'television' of their day, their media coverage of Queen Victoria's Colonial Small Wars bringing home to the public the faces and the places of each campaign. The Anglo-Zulu War was no exception, and by use of engravings – some based on actual photographs – the newspapers were able to convey a perception of the campaign to the public at large.

All the illustrations used in this book are from the author's own collection.—J.Y.

To the memory of those brave men who died
in the Anglo-Zulu War of 1879, irrespective
of their creed or colour and whether black or white,
Briton, Zulu or Boer, or Imperial or Colonial.
This book is a tribute to them all.

I

Ultimatum and Invasion

'Strange official mistake in geography – to have
placed Chelmsford in Africa' – *Punch*

IN MARCH 1878 Major-General the Honourable Frederic
Augustus Thesiger arrived in South Africa to command Her
Majesty Queen Victoria's armed forces. The command carried
a local rank of lieutenant-general and Thesiger was to replace
Lieutenant-General Arthur Cunynghame who had been recalled from his position as a consequence of political pressure.
Thesiger was the eldest son of the 1st Baron Chelmsford, a
former Lord Chancellor. He had seen active service in the
Crimea, the Indian Mutiny and the Abyssinian Campaign and
he had also held various staff appointments in Great Britain
and the Empire.

As a soldier, Thesiger was a servant of the Crown, and in
South Africa the Crown was personified by the Governor of
Cape Colony and High Commissioner for Native Affairs, Sir
Henry Bartle Edward Frere. Frere was an outstanding civil
servant who had performed sterling work on the Indian
sub-continent. In October 1876 he had been directed to South
Africa by the then Colonial Secretary, Lord Carnarvon; his
main task was to bring about a confederation of the frag-
mented South African Colonies and States. First to fall into the
Confederation was the Boer Republic of the Transvaal,
annexed in April 1877. With the acquisition of the Transvaal
the Government inherited a dispute over a strip of border
territory between the Boers and the fiercely independent kingdom of Zululand, ruled by King Cetshwayo.

In December 1877 Frere launched an unprecedented propaganda campaign against Cetshwayo. Labelling the king a despot and his army man-slaying gladiators, Frere was trying his hardest to provoke a war with the Zulu. However, the British forces in South Africa were already embroiled in the Ninth Cape Frontier War.

In March 1878, almost coinciding with Thesiger's arrival, a commission was formed to unravel the complexities of the Boer-Zulu border dispute. Frere bombarded London (where in January Sir Michael Hicks Beach had replaced Lord Carnarvon as Colonial Secretary) with numerous despatches which did nothing but malign Cetshwayo and his intentions. For example, on 3rd June 1878 he wrote: 'It is quite clear that the war spirit is abroad . . . I have no doubt and never had that the Zulus mean mischief.'

The following month an event occurred that added credence to Frere's cause. One of the wives of the powerful border chieftain Sihayo kaXongo had become pregnant by another man and fled with her lover into Natal. Shortly afterwards another unfaithful wife, also pregnant, followed. The first wife took up residence in the kraal of a border policeman, Mswaglele.

Mehlokazulu, chief son of Sihayo, outraged by the behaviour of his father's wives, decided to take action against them and on 28th July led a large force of men across the Buffalo River and into Natal. Armed Zulus, now in a British colony, made for Mswaglele's kraal and surrounded it, demanding the return of the wives. Desperately outnumbered, the border police could offer no real resistance and one of the wives was dragged out of the hut in which she was hiding. She was manhandled back across the Buffalo and into Zululand where she was put to death. That same night the incursion was renewed and the other miscreant wife met the same fate.

The Natal Government sought reparation and demanded the surrender of the ringleaders of the raid but Sihayo refused to comply with the demand. He merely offered to pay a fine of cattle which King Cetshwayo had levied on him for the

SIR HENRY BARTLE EDWARD FRERE, GOVERNOR OF CAPE COLONY
AND HIGH COMMISSIONER FOR NATIVE AFFAIRS

15

SIR MICHAEL HICKS BEACH, COLONIAL SECRETARY

16

KING CETSHWAYO KAMPANDE. HE IS DEPICTED IN THIS ENGRAVING
WEARING THE TINSEL CROWN GIVEN TO HIM BY THE BRITISH AT THE
TIME OF HIS 'CORONATION' IN 1873

17

FRERE'S ULTIMATUM BEING DELIVERED TO KING CETSHWAYO'S
IZINDUNA, HIS STATE OFFICIALS. THE TERM 'IZINDUNA' (SINGULAR: 'INDUNA')
ALSO APPLIED TO ZULU MILITARY COMMANDERS.

NUMBER 3 COLUMN CROSSING THE BUFFALO RIVER AT RORKE'S DRIFT, SATURDAY, 11TH JANUARY 1879. NOTE THE NATIVES PULLING THE HAWSER OF THE PONT, IN ORDER TO FERRY THE TROOPS ACROSS.

incursion. This offer, however, did not impress the Natal government and it was duly dismissed.

On 10th September Frere sent a cable to London requesting military reinforcements for South Africa to which Hicks Beach replied to the effect that discussion as a means of arbitration would be better than a military solution.

By mid-1878 with the successful conclusion of the Ninth Frontier War, Thesiger, coerced it would appear by Frere, turned his attentions to the Zulu. He had prepared his famous pamphlet *The Zulu Army, and Zulu Headmen*, drawn from information collated by a border agent, Mr H.B. Fynney, and which contained details of the Zulu regimental system, command structure and tactics. Future events would cause this pamphlet to be revised.

In mid-September another incident strengthened Frere's cause. A surveyor of the Colonial Engineer's Office, Mr (or in some accounts Lieutenant) D. Smith, accompanied by a trader named Deighton, was conducting a survey of the road leading between Greytown and Fort Buckingham. Whilst standing on a rock near to the middle Drift of the Tugela River, they were accosted by a number of Zulus who detained them for about an hour and relieved them of some possessions.

On 17th October, Hicks Beach despatched a reply to Frere's cable informing him that the Government had acquiesced in part to his request and were sending out six 'special service' officers and would probably be prepared, if hostilities broke out, to send more troops. He went on to say:

Her Majesty's Government are, however, not prepared to comply with the request for a reinforcement of troops. All the information that has hitherto reached them, with respect to the position of affairs in Zululand, appears to them to justify a confident hope that by the exercise of prudence, and by meeting the Zulus in a spirit of forbearance and reasonable comprise, it will be possible to avert the very serious evil of a war with Cetewayo [sic]; and they cannot but think that the forces now at your disposal in South Africa, together

20

with the additional officers about to be sent, should suffice to meet any other emergency that may arise without a further increase to the Imperial troops.

It appears that the Colonial Secretary was blissfully unaware that Thesiger had already drawn up his invasion plans in readiness.

Early in October, another string was added to Frere's bow. Mbilini, a renegade Swazi prince who sought refuge in Zulu-

LIEUTENANT-GENERAL
LORD CHELMSFORD

land, effected a raid across the Pongola River and killed several Swazis on British territory. From Pietermaritzburg, Frere and Lord Chelmsford (Thesiger succeeded his father to the title in October) set about mobilising their forces. In addition, Chelmsford had also gained permission, albeit reluctant, from the Lieutenant-Governor of Natal, Sir Henry Ernest Bulwer, to raise a level of 7,000 natives – thus the Natal Native Contingent was formed. In addition, the local volunteer forces were called out and mustered in readiness.

In November, King Cetshwayo was informed that a great inDaba had been convened for Wednesday, 11th December 1878 on the Natal bank of the Lower Drift of the Tugela. Here the findings of the Boundary Commission would be announced. Cetshwayo directed three izinDuna to receive the findings. They were accompanied to the inDaba by a number of petty chieftains, their retainers and John Dunn, a 'white Zulu' and confidant of Cetshwayo, where they were informed that the Commission had found in favour of the Zulu, but with certain stipulations: that if any Boers remained in the territory they would come under the protection of a British Resident in Utrecht; those who opted to leave were to be remunerated by the Zulu. The meeting was adjourned for half an hour and when it was reconvened the Zulu emissaries were regaled by the reading of an ultimatum from Frere, the main points of which were:

1. The ringleaders of the incursion across the Buffalo should be surrendered for trial under British law, and a fine of 500 cattle paid for the violation.

2. A fine of 100 cattle should be paid for the offence committed against Smith and Deighton.

   [These two stipulations were to be met by Tuesday, 31st December 1878.]

3. Mbilini and his confederates were to be surrendered for trial for their incursion across the Pongola.

4. That the Zulu army should be disbanded and only brought together with the permission of a Great Council of the Zulu nation which would be under the auspice of the British Government.

5. That Zulus were to be allowed to marry on reaching maturity without requiring the King's consent.

6. The system of justice should be reformed and that accused persons had the right of personal trial.

7. A British Resident should be received at the Zulu capital, Ulundi.

8. All missionaries and native converts who had fled Zululand for fear of persecution should be allowed to return to their mission stations.

9. If any missionary or other European should be involved in a dispute, the matter should be heard by the king and in the presence of the Resident, and that any sentence of expulsion from Zululand could not be carried out without the Resident's approval.

[These seven demands were to be fulfilled within thirty days.]

Frere was endeavouring to impose his demands on King Cetshwayo – demands he knew the king could not, and would not, accept and Chelmsford mustered his forces in readiness for what now was inevitable. His plan of defence of the colony of Natal was the invasion of Zululand. Three main columns and two reserve columns were formed:

No. 1 Column, commanded by Colonel C.K. Pearson, 3rd (East Kent) Regiment of Foot ('The Buffs'), situated at the Lower Drift of the Tugela River.

No. 2 Column, commanded by Brevet Colonel A.W. Durnford, Royal Engineers, situated on reserve at the Middle Drift.

No. 3 Column, commanded by Colonel R.T. Glyn, 1st Battalion, 24th (2nd Warwickshires) Regiment of Foot, situated at Rorke's Drift.

No. 4 Column, commanded by Brevet Colonel H.E. Wood, VC, 90th (Perthshire Volunteers) Light Infantry, situated at Bemba's Kop.

No. 5 Column, commanded by Colonel H. Rowlands, VC, late of 34th Regiment of Foot, situated on reserve at Luneburg.

The three attacking columns, Nos. 1, 3 and 4, were approximately fifty miles from Chelmsford's objective, King Cetshwayo's capital of Ulundi.

The twenty days stipulated for the first two demands elapsed with no reply from King Cetshwayo. Accordingly, on Saturday, 4th January 1879 from Government House, Pietermaritzburg His Excellency Sir Henry Bartle Edward Frere forwarded the following communiqué to his superior in London:

Sir

I have the honour to forward the Notification I have felt obliged to issue, declaring a state of war between Her Majesty's Government and the Zulu King, consequent on his non-compliance with the demands made on him, urging reparation and redress for violations of British territory.

I have, & C.

(signed) H.B. Frere

Her Majesty's High Commissioner

Without the sanction of the Home Government Frere had declared war on an independent, albeit tribal, kingdom: a war that would be conducted by Frere's willing subordinate – Lieutenant-General Lord Chelmsford. The thirty days stipulated in the ultimatum had expired and in the early hours of Saturday, 11th January 1879, Lord Chelmsford attached his headquarters to No. 3 Column and supervised their crossing of the Buffalo at Rorke's Drift.

British troops were now in Zululand. The invasion was under way.

II

The Assault on the Kraals of Sihayo kaXongo Sunday, 12th January 1879

'By whose order the white impi had come there . . . ?' – *A Zulu Defender*

THE ADVANCE of No. 3 Column into Zululand was barred on the mountain kraals of the chieftain Sihayo kaXongo, which were situated at the western edge of the Nquthu plateau, near to the Batse River. As Sihayo had been used by Bartle Frere as one of his excuses for the invasion of Zululand, hostility was inevitable. Having taken up positions before the main kraal of Sihayo, at about 7.15 a.m. the British were challenged by a Zulu. He asked by whose order the white impi had come there, and whether they were enemies? Captain R. Duncombe, Natal Native Contingent, a Zulu linguist, is attributed with the reply, 'By the orders of the Great White Queen!'

At 7.30 a.m. the first Zulu shot wounded a native of the NNC. The British then advanced and the Zulu defenders retired into a series of caves, from which they fired upon the advancing British troops, and pushed boulders down the slopes in a futile attempt to stop the advance. The caves were stormed by Hamilton-Browne's No. 8 Company, 1st Battalion, 3rd Regiment, Natal Native Contingent, themselves expatriate Zulus, who engaged the defenders in hand to hand combat. Their fine performance was sadly not followed by all the NNC troops, some of whom had wavered in the attack.

Meanwhile, the four companies of the 1st Battalion, 24th (2nd Warwickshires) Regiment of Foot, under Captain W.

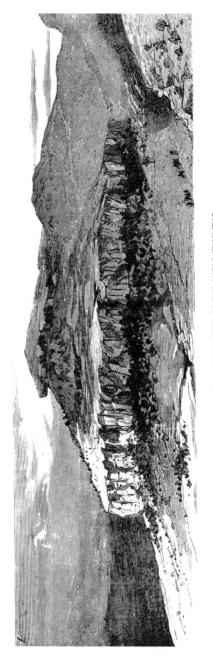

THE SCENE OF THE FIRST BATTLE OF THE ANGLO-ZULU WAR,
SIHAYO KAXONGO'S KRAAL ON THE BATSE RIVER. TO THE BOTTOM
RIGHT, HUTS OF THE KRAAL HAVE BEEN PUT TO THE TORCH.

Degacher, had surmounted the heights above the kraal in an attempt to prevent the Zulus from escaping. However, several had already evaded the encircling British and were pursued by British mounted troops. A reserve force comprised of the 2nd Battalion of the 24th (2nd Warwickshires) Regiment of Foot took possession of a secondary kraal, only to find it deserted.

Sihayo's kraals were burnt and his cattle herd taken as booty. One of his sons, Mkumbikazulu, had died in the action but British retribution was not to be fully exacted for Sihayo was absent at Ulundi. The action was concluded by 9.30 a.m.

The Composition of the British Force

Colonel R.T. Glyn, 1st Battalion, 24th (2nd Warwickshires) Regiment of Foot, commanding:

Staff Officer: Lieutenant N.J.A. Coghill, 1st Battalion, 24th (2nd Warwickshires) Regiment of Foot

1st Battalion 3rd Regiment Natal Native Contingent

Brevet Lieutenant-Colonel W. Black, 2/24th and Commandant G. Hamilton-Browne, temporarily commanding:

Staff Officer: Lieutenant H.C. Harford, 99th Duke of Edinburgh's (Lanarkshire) Regiment of Foot

and 850 officers and other ranks

1st Battalion, 24th (2nd Warwickshires) Regiment of Foot
Four companies commanded by Captain W. Degacher
Captains: G.V. Wardell; R. Younghusband
Lieutenants: T. Melvill (Adjutant); F.P. Porteous; C.W. Cavaye; G.F.J. Hodson; C.J. Atkinson
Second Lieutenant E.H. Dyson
Paymaster F.F. White
Quartermaster J. Pullen
and approximately 400 other ranks

Lieutenant-Colonel (Local Rank) J.C. Russell, 12th (Prince of Wales' Royal) Lancers, commanding the mounted detachment comprising:

CAPTAIN W. DEGACHER,
24TH FOOT

CAPTAIN G.V. WARDELL,
24TH FOOT

1st Squadron, Mounted Infantry
Commanded by Lieutenant E.S. Browne, 1st Battalion, 24th (2nd
  Warwickshires) Regiment of Foot

Natal Mounted Police
80 men under Inspector G. Mansell

Natal Carbineers
30 men under Captain T. Shepstone

Buffalo Border Guard and Newcastle Mounted Rifles
35 men under Captain C.R. Bradstreet

British and Colonial Casualties

KILLED IN ACTION
Natal Native Contingent
Two natives (names unknown)

WOUNDED IN ACTION
1st Battalion, 3rd Regiment, Natal Native Contingent
Lieutenant T. Purvis, severely wounded
Corporal J.H. Mayer, slightly wounded
15 native other ranks (names and severity of wounds unknown)

Zulu Casualties

About 30 killed, four wounded and ten prisoners taken.

III

The Battle of Nyezane
Wednesday, 22nd January 1879

'We gave them a good whacking'
*— Colour-Sgt J.W. Burnett, 99th Duke of Edinburgh's
(Lanarkshire) Regiment of Foot*

COLONEL C.K. PEARSON of the 2nd Battalion, 3rd (East Kent) Regiment of Foot ('The Buffs'), commanding No. 1 Column had crossed the Tugela on 11th January 1879. He set about establishing a fortification on the Zulu bank which became known as Fort 'Tenedos'. On the 18th Pearson cautiously advanced into Zululand, with half of his column. His mounted troops (2nd Squadron Mounted Infantry, Natal Hussars, Durban Mounted Rifles, Alexandra Mounted Rifles, Stanger Mounted Rifles and Victoria Mounted Rifles) skirted the line of advance. The remainder of the column commanded by Lieutenant-Colonel W.H.D.R. Welman, 99th Duke of Edinburgh's (Lanarkshire) Regiment of Foot, followed on the 19th.

On Wednesday, 22nd January at about 8 a.m. the column had crossed the Nyezane River, and Pearson was seeking a suitable halting place.

A company of the 1st Battalion, 2nd Regiment of the Natal Native Contingent, commanded by Captain A.F. Hart, 31st (Huntingdonshire) Regiment of Foot, reconnoitred the hills ahead; the mounted patrols had been ordered to return to Colonel Pearson for further orders. Hart's men came under heavy gunfire from Zulus positioned on the dominating hills. A large body of Zulus appeared on the crest of the hills. Unable to meet the challenge, the NNC were ordered to withdraw but

30

in the confusion the withdrawal turned into a rout. Two officers and four non-commissioned officers of the NNC, abandoned to their fate by their men, fell in a desperate stand against the advancing Zulus.

Pearson threw out two companies of the 3rd Foot and a detachment of the Naval Landing Brigade of HMS *Active*, supported by two cannon of the 11th Battery, 7th Brigade, Royal Artillery and Naval Brigade rocket battery, in an effort to stem the advance of the Zulu left horn. The Zulu centre came to within 400 yards of the British line before the two cannon diverted their attention. A Gatling gun, commanded by Midshipman L.C. Coker of the *Active*, was brought into action, scything down the oncoming Zulus.

Captain W.R.C. Wynne deployed the 2nd (Field) Company, Royal Engineers as Infantry, in support of the Mounted Infantry and Colonial Volunteers, the Victoria and Stanger Mounted Rifles and the Natal Hussars, who were engaging the Zulu right horn. Two half companies of the 3rd Foot and the 99th Foot respectively joined the fray, having been ordered forward by Welman who was advancing with his section of the column.

Commander H.J.F. Campbell of the *Active* observed a Zulu outflanking manoeuvre and charged at the Zulu centre with his ship's landing brigade, a company of the 3rd Foot and the Europeans of the 1st/2nd NNC. The ferocity of the attack drove the Zulus from their positions; demoralised, they fled the field. The time was 9.30 a.m.

The Composition of the British Force

Colonel C.K. Pearson, 2nd Battalion, 3rd (East Kent) Regiment of Foot ('The Buffs'), commanding:

Staff: Brevet Colonel F.W.E.F. Walker, Scots Guards; Brevet Major E. Pelly Clarke, 103rd (Royal Bombay Fusiliers) Regiment of Foot, Director of Transport; Captain H.G. Macgregor, 29th (Worcestershire) Regiment of Foot; Lieutenant H.R. Knight, 2nd/3rd Foot, orderly officer and ADC to Colonel Pearson; Lieutenant J.

THE NAVAL LANDING BRIGADE FROM HMS *ACTIVE*; IN THE LE▮
AND ON THE EXTREME RIGHT IS THE BRIGADE'S GATLING GUN. THE NEGRO▮
ROYAL NAVY FOR THEIR SKILLED SEAMANSHIP IN LANDING SMALL CRAF▮

REGROUND IS ONE OF THE TWO 7 LB CANNON OF THE BRIGADE
HIND THE CANNON ARE COASTAL WEST AFRICANS, RECRUITED INTO THE
IEY WERE REFERRED TO BY THE SHIP'S COMPANY AS 'KROOMEN'.

COMMANDANT W.J. NETTLETON (SEATED CENTRE),
COMMANDER OF 2ND BATTALION, 2ND REGIMENT, NATAL NATIVE
CONTINGENT. THE ENGRAVING ACTUALLY DATES FROM 1880 BUT DOUBTLESS
SOME OF THE OFFICERS DEPICTED SERVED UNDER
NETTLETON IN 1879.

Thirkill, 88th (Connaught Rangers) Regiment of Foot, Transport Duties; Assistant Commissary E.L.B. Kevill-Davies, (Transport Duties), Assistant Commissary B. Heygate (supply officer), Sub-Assistant Commissary W. Wishart, Commissariat and Transport Department.

11th Battery, 7th Brigade, Royal Artillery
Two 7 lb cannon and 22 men commanded by Lieutenant W.N. Lloyd

CAPTAIN W.R.C. WYNNE,
2ND (FIELD) COMPANY,
ROYAL ENGINEERS

2nd (Field) Company, Royal Engineers
85 men, Captain D.C. Courtney, Lieutenant T.R. Main and Lieutenant H.B. Willock commanded by Captain W.R.C. Wynne

2nd Battalion, 3rd (East Kent) Regiment of Foot ('The Buffs')
Five companies commanded by Lieutenant-Colonel H. Parnell
Captains: H.J.M. Williams; J.E. Forster; H.D. Harrison; G.A. Alexander; W.H. Wyld; H.W. Maclear; R.W. M'G. Martin; J.B. Backhouse
Lieutenants: H.C. Somerset (Adjutant); C.H. Gordon; D.F. Lewis; J.

Hughes; C.E. Mason; H.J.J. Middleton; H. Blackburn; C.L. Connellan; J.C.L. Knight-Bruce; C.B. Vyvyan
2nd Lieutenant G.R.J. Evelyn
Quartermaster W.G. Morgan
and 400 other ranks

99th Duke of Edinburgh's (Lanarkshire) Regiment of Foot
Two companies commanded by Lieutenant-Colonel W.H.D.R. Welman
Brevet Lieutenant-Colonel C. Coates
Captains: F.L. Story; C.H.S. Kennedy
Lieutenants: A.W. Turner; T.G. Johnson; A.S.F. Davison; G.C.J. Johnson; C.H. Alexander
Quartermaster J. Bateman
and 160 other ranks

Naval Landing Brigade from HMS Active
Detachment, including two 7 lb cannon, a Gatling gun and rocket tube, commanded by Commander H.J.F. Campbell
Commander (Gunnery) R.W. Craigie
Lieutenants: W. des V. Hamilton; T.G. Fraser; J.G. Hengh
Fleet-Surgeon H.F. Norbury
Surgeon W. Thompson
Midshipman L.C. Coker, Gatling gun commander
Chief Boatswain J. Cotter, Rocket Battery commander
Captain T.W. Dowding, Royal Marine Light Infantry
128 ratings and marines

2nd Squadron Mounted Infantry
Squadron commanded by Brevet Major P.H.S. Barrow, 19th Hussars
Lieutenants: E.R. Courtenay, 20th Hussars; H. de C. Rawlins, 90th Light Infantry; H.W. Rowden, 99th Foot
115 other ranks drawn from various regular units

The Natal Hussars
One officer and 37 other ranks commanded by Captain P. Norton

The Stanger Mounted Rifles
One officer and 35 other ranks, commanded by Captain F. Addison

The Victoria Mounted Rifles
One officer and 45 other ranks, commanded by Captain C. Saner

2nd Regiment Natal Native Contingent
Commanded by Major S. Graves, 2nd Battalion, 3rd Regiment of
  Foot
Staff Officer: Captain A.F. Hart, 31st (Huntingdonshire) Regiment
  of Foot

1st Battalion, 2nd Regiment, Natal Native Contingent
Personally commanded by Major Graves comprising 28 officers and
  800 other ranks

2nd Battalion, 2nd Regiment, Natal Native Contingent
Commanded by Commandant W.J. Nettleton, comprising 27
  officers and 800 other ranks

No. 2 Company Natal Native Pioneers
60 other ranks commanded by Captain G.K.E. Beddoes and Lieutenant Porrington

British and Colonial Casualties

KILLED IN ACTION
2nd Battalion, 3rd Regiment of Foot ('The Buffs')
Privates: J. Bough; J. Kelleher

2nd Battalion, 2nd Regiment Natal Native Contingent
Lieutenants: G. Plattner; J.L. Raines
Sergeant E. Unger
Corporals: C. Goesh; E. Miller; W. Lieper
Four unnamed native privates

WOUNDED IN ACTION
2nd Battalion, 3rd (East Kent) Regiment of Foot ('The Buffs')
Private F. Clifford, severely wounded
Private J. Cordell, dangerously wounded
Private P. Dunne, mortally wounded – died of wounds 23rd January
  1879
Private F. Smith, severely wounded
Private H. Walker, severely wounded

2nd Squadron Mounted Infantry
(Listed by parent units)

90th (Perthshire Volunteers) Light Infantry
Quartermaster-Sergeant F. Kelly, severely wounded

2nd Battalion, 24th (2nd Warwickshires) Regiment of Foot
Private (Musketry Instructor) W. Davenport, dangerously wounded
(Compiler's Note: Private W. Davenport died as a result of illness on
3rd May 1879. I am not in a position to attribute this to the wound or
its consequences.)

LIEUTENANT
J.L. RAINES,
2ND/2ND NNC

HMS Active
Petty Officer E. White, slightly wounded
Stoker 'Sergeant' (2nd Class) T. Butler, slightly wounded
Able Seaman H.D. Gosling, severely wounded
Ordinary Seaman G. Berryman, severely wounded
Ordinary Seaman G. Doran, dangerously wounded
Krooman Duckleweis, slightly wounded
Krooman Jack Ropeyarn, slightly wounded
Krooman Jack Lewis, slightly wounded

1st Battalion, 2nd Regiment of Natal Native Contingent
Lieutenant H. Webb, slightly wounded
Sergeant O. Heydenberg, dangerously wounded
(Sergeant Heydenberg's wound necessitated the amputation of a leg. On 26th January 1879 he died. This compiler is not able to establish whether death was of a *direct* result of the wound or from trauma.)

Zulu Casualties

Some 400 dead found on the battlefield

IV

The Debacle at Isandlwana
Wednesday, 22nd January 1879

*'I regret to have to report a very disastrous
engagement . . .' – Lieutenant-General
The Lord Chelmsford*

N O. 3 COLUMN established camp at the base of the mountain of Isandlwana on 20th January. Lord Chelmsford
did not have the wagons laagered in a defensive position,
contrary to his own instructions, for he felt that the Zulu threat
lay nearer to the royal kraal at Ulundi. On the 21st he ordered
a two pronged reconnaissance to probe the stronghold of
Matshana kaMondisa. Commandant Rupert Lonsdale took
two NNC battalions eastwards on one route, whilst Major J.
Dartnell took eighty of his Natal Mounted Police, together
with fifty mounted volunteers, on another.

In the late afternoon, Dartnell made contact with the forces
of Matshana and sought assistance from Lord Chelmsford. At
4.30 a.m. on Wednesday, the 22nd, Chelmsford divided No. 3
Column in order to reinforce Dartnell taking with him six
companies of the 2/24th, four cannon from N/5 Brigade RA
and most of the mounted infantry squadron. As he left Isandlwana, Chelmsford had a hurried note penned to Brevet
Colonel A.W. Durnford, RE, who was encamped at Rorke's
Drift with his No. 2 Column, instructing him to reinforce the
remaining troops at Isandlwana.

The command of the encampment now devolved to Brevet
Lieutenant-Colonel H.B. Pulleine 1/24th. At 8 a.m. Zulus
were sighted advancing towards the encampment from the
north-west. Pulleine recalled his regular infantry picquets who

joined the rest of the infantry in forming up before the camp. Two companies of the NNC remained on picquet whilst a detachment of the Natal Carbineers remained on vedette duty.

At 10.30 a.m. the camp was reinforced by the arrival of Durnford's force and at about 11 a.m. Durnford sent out a detachment of his Natal Native Horse to clear the Zulus occupying the high ground. At 11.30 Durnford received information that the Zulus were falling back eastwards. To prevent a linking of the Zulu force near Isandlwana and those

MAJOR J. DARTNELL,
NATAL MOUNTED POLICE

currently opposing Chelmsford, Durnford led out two troops of NNH and gave orders for No. 5 Company of 2nd/3rd NNC and the rocket battery, under Brevet Major Russell, to act in his support.

The NNH under Lieutenant C. Raw then encountered the concealed Zulu impi, numbering approximately 25,000 men. The Zulu commanders had not intended to attack the encampment that day, but now the circumstances had changed. The young men of the umCijo, eager to fight, rose up and charged.

NATIVE HORSEMEN ENCAMPING. ALTHOUGH THIS ENGRAVING IS ACTUALLY FROM THE NINTH CAPE FRONTIER WAR, IT GIVES A GOOD IMPRESSION OF THE DRESS OF THE TROOPS SERVING IN THE NATAL NATIVE HORSE.

A CONTEMPORARY SKETCH PLAN OF THE BATTLE OF ISANDLWANA

THE SURVIVORS OF ISANDLWANA, FORDING THE SWOLLEN WATERS OF
THE BUFFALO RIVER AT FUGITIVES' DRIFT AND RELENTLESSLY PURSUED BY ZULU

THE MEMORIAL CROSS TO LIEUTENANTS MELVILL AND COGHILL

The izinDuna tried to stem the tide but only succeeded in keeping the uNdi 'corps' in reserve. The Zulu formed into a crescent formation and the die for disaster was cast.

No. 5 Company 2nd/3rd NNC, under Captain A.J. Barry, broke, and the rocket battery was overwhelmed. Both Durnford and Shepstone waged a fighting retreat. Durnford was reinforced by detachments of the Natal Mounted Police, Natal Carbineers, Newcastle Mounted Rifles and the Buffalo Border Guard, in a desperate attempt to turn the Zulu left horn. At

BREVET COLONEL
A.W. DURNFORD,
ROYAL ENGINEERS

12.15 p.m. the regular British infantry fell in and were deployed in skirmish lines supported by the two cannon of N/5 RA, NNH and detachments of the NNC.

The volley firing of the 24th succeeded in checking the Zulu advance. Durnford's troops, however, were now desperately short of ammunition and were compelled to abandon their position. Lieutenant C. Pope, commanding 'G' Company 2/24th, was endeavouring to reinforce Durnford but he was forced to retire. Seized by fear the companies of the NNC, who were in the firing line, decamped, thus leaving a yawning gap in the line and compelling Pulleine to draw his line back on the encampment. A reserve company of the 1st/3rd NNC fled without engaging the Zulus. The time was now about 1.15 p.m. and through sheer weight of numbers the Zulus gained the encampment. Organised resistance dwindled to isolated pockets.

Seeing all was lost, Pulleine ordered his adjutant, Lieutenant Teignmouth Melvill, to save the Queen's Colour of the 1/24th.

BREVET LIEUTENANT-
COLONEL H.B. PULLEINE,
1ST/24TH FOOT

The battle may have been lost but, hopefully, honour might still be saved.

Melvill joined the stream of fugitives towards the Buffalo River. Soon, their fate sealed, the British were overwhelmed. The fugitives were pursued and came under attack from the uNdi 'corps', who harried them to the banks of the Buffalo. In the torrent of the river Melvill lost his grasp on the Colour, but he gained the Natal bank with the assistance of Lieutenant Nevill Coghill. Together they climbed the steep embankment only to be overtaken by Zulus and killed. The field of Isand-lwana was now in the hands of the victorious Zulus. The time was about 2.30 p.m.

The Composition of the British Force

NO. 2 COLUMN (part)

Brevet Colonel A.W. Durnford, Royal Engineers, commanding:

Staff: Captain G.J.P. Shepstone, Natal Native Horse, Political Assistant; Lieutenant W.F.D. Cochrane, 32nd (Cornwall) Light Infantry, transport officer; and 2nd Corporal N. Mansfield, 7th (Field) Company, RE

Rocket Battery: commanded by Brevet Major F.B. Russell, 11th Battery, 7th Brigade, Royal Artillery, comprising one acting bombardier, N/5 RA and eight other ranks 1/24th Foot.

Natal Native Horse: Captain W. Barton
(Each troop comprised of approximately 50 men)
No. 1 Troop, Sikali's Horse under Lieutenant C. Raw
No. 2 Troop, Sikali's Horse under Lieutenant J.A. Roberts
No. 3 Troop, Sikali's Horse under Lieutenant R.W. Vause
Hlubi Troop under Lieutenant A.F. Henderson
Edendale Troop under Lieutenant H.D. Davies

1st Battalion, 1st Regiment NNC
Companies 'D' and 'E' (about 240 men)

NO. 3 COLUMN (part)

Brevet Lieutenant-Colonel H.B. Pulleine, 1st Battalion, 24th (2nd Warwickshires) Regiment of Foot, commanding:

Staff: Captain A.C. Gardner, 14th (King's) Hussars, general duties; Captain E. Essex, 75th (Stirlingshire) Regiment of Foot, Director of Transport; Lieutenant F.H. MacDowell, RE; Lieutenant N.J.A. Coghill, 1/24th Foot, orderly officer to Colonel Glyn; Lieutenant H.L. Smith-Dorrien, 95th (Derbyshire) Regiment of Foot, transport duties; Surgeon-Major P. Shepherd, MB, Army Medical Department; Mr J.A. Brickhill, interpreter; 13 men.

'N' Battery, 5th Brigade Royal Artillery
Two 7 lb cannon and 70 men commanded by Brevet Major S. Smith
and Lieutenant H.T. Curling

5th (Field) Company Royal Engineers
Detachment of a corporal and three sappers

1st Battalion, 24th (2nd Warwickshires) Regiment of Foot
Headquarters and five companies
Acting Major W. Degacher commanding:
Lieutenant T. Melvill, Adjutant

LIEUTENANT
H.L. SMITH-DORRIEN,
95TH FOOT

'A' Company under Lieutenant F.P. Porteous
'C' Company under Captain R. Younghusband and Lieutenant
   G.F.J. Hodson
'E' Company under Lieutenant C.W. Cavaye and Second Lieutenant
   E.H. Dyson
'F' Company under Captain W.E. Mostyn, Lieutenants E.O. Anstey
   and J.P. Daly
'H' Company under Captain G.V. Wardell and Lieutenant C.J.
   Atkinson
Paymaster F.F. White, Quartermaster J. Pullen and 402 other ranks

2nd Battalion, 24th (2nd Warwickshires) Regiment of Foot
One company and other details
'G' Company under Lieutenants C.D'A. Pope and F. Godwin-Austen. Lieutenant H.J. Dyer, Adjutant; Sub-Lieutenant T.L.G. Griffith, Transport Duties; Quartermaster E. Bloomfield; and 170 men

90th (Perthshire Volunteers) Light Infantry
Six men seconded to 1/24th Foot
Details of the Army Hospital Corps and Army Service Corps

LIEUTENANT
F.P. PORTEOUS,
1ST/24TH FOOT

1st Squadron Mounted Infantry
Detachment of 20 other ranks

Natal Mounted Police
34 men

Natal Carbineers
Two officers, 27 other ranks

Newcastle Mounted Rifles
Two officers, 12 other ranks

Buffalo Border Guard
One officer, seven other ranks

1st Battalion, 3rd Regiment, Natal Native Contingent
Companies No. 6 and No. 9; nine officers and approximately 200 men

2nd Battalion, 3rd Regiment Natal Native Contingent
Companies No. 4 and No. 5; 11 officers and approximately 200 men

BREVET MAJOR
F.B. RUSSELL, 11TH/7TH
ROYAL ARTILLERY

No. 1 Company, Natal Native Pioneer Corps
Detachment of one officer and 10 men

British and Colonial Casualties

KILLED IN ACTION
NO. 2 COLUMN (PART) EUROPEANS
Brevet Colonel A.W. Durnford, Royal Engineers
Staff: Captain G.J.P. Shepstone, Natal Native Horse, 2nd Corporal
  N. Mansfield, 7th (Field) Company, Royal Engineers
Rocket Battery: Brevet Major F.B. Russell, 11th Battery, 7th Bri-
  gade, Royal Artillery; Private C. Mahoney, 1st Battalion, 24th
  (2nd Warwickshires) Regiment of Foot

(N.B. As the records of the 24th Foot were lost, the four other 1/24th casualties are included in the roll of the 1/24th)

Natal Native Horse
Lieutenant J.A. Roberts, No. 2 Troop, Sikali's Horse (killed by artillery fire from N/5 RA)

1st Battalion, 1st Regiment NNC
Lieutenants: N.D. Black and Lister

LIEUTENANT N.D. BLACK
1ST/1ST NNC

NO. 3 COLUMN (PART) EUROPEANS

Brevet Lieutenant-Colonel H.B. Pulleine, 1st Battalion, 24th (2nd Warwickshires) Regiment of Foot

Staff: Lieutenant F.H. MacDowell, RE; Lieutenant N.J.A. Coghill, VC, 1/24th Foot; Surgeon Major P. Shepherd, Army Medical Department; Colour-Sergeant M.C. Keane, Staff Corps; Private W. Hough, 1/24th, Colonel Glyn's cook; Private J. Williamson, 2/24th Foot and Private M. Fitzpatrick, 25th Foot, soldier servants; Private G. Watson, 31st Foot, General's servant. Sergeant H. Thompson, 80th Foot (seconded 2/24th Foot); Farrier & Carriage Smith Corporal A. Wright, ASC; Signalman 1st Class

LIEUTENANT
F.H. MACDOWELL,
ROYAL ENGINEERS

SURGEON MAJOR
P. SHEPHERD, ARMY
MEDICAL DEPARTMENT

W.H. Aynsley, HMS *Active*; Mr Laparra, General's cook; W. Popworth, civilian servant to Captain A.C. Gardener, 14th Hussars; R. Turner, civilian servant to Captain H.H. Parr, 13th Light Infantry; 'Boy' Green, civilian servant to Surgeon Major P. Shepherd, AMD

'N' Battery, 5th Brigade, Royal Artillery
Brevet Major S. Smith
Sergeant W. Edwards
Farrier Sergeant R. Whinham

BREVET MAJOR
S. SMITH, 'N'/5TH
ROYAL ARTILLERY

Corporals: H.R. Bailey; W. Cooper; J. Langridge
Acting Bombardiers: J. Aylett; T. Boswell; J.L. Lequay; J. McDonnell; T. Nash; J. Parker
Collar-maker T. Shepherd
Shoeing-smith T. Elliott
Gunners: F. Beach; T. Berry; J. Burke; J. Byrne; S.J. Cochrane; R. Collins; J. Connelly; I. Davies; W. Dickens; T. Harrison; J. Hicks; E.G. James; C. King; J. Lamb; M.R. McGregor; J. Meade; T. Miller; D. O'Neil; H. Page; A. Redman; J. Reed; J. Regan; W.

Roscoe; J. Smythe; J. Stevenson; R. Williams; T. Wilson; W. Wilson; A. Woolacott

Drivers: W. Adams; H. Allen; W. Barron; C. Bishop; J. Brooks; T. Bruce; T. Clark; H. Cowley; J. Daley; W. Hiatt; J. Hutchings; J.W. Jones; L. Joyce; J. Marchant; W. Marshall; G. McKeown; F.A. Murphy; C. Spread

5th (Field) Company, Royal Engineers
Corporal W. Gamble
Sappers: H. Cuthbert; J. McLaren; M. Wheatley

CAPTAIN W.E. MOSTYN,
1ST/24TH FOOT

1st Battalion, 24th (2nd Warwickshires) Regiment of Foot
Acting Major W. Degacher
Captains: W.E. Mostyn; R. Younghusband; G.V. Wardell
Lieutenants: E.O. Anstey; C.J. Atkinson; C.W. Cavaye; J.P. Daly; G.F.J. Hodson; T. Melvill, vc; F.P. Porteous
Second-Lieutenant E.H. Dyson
Paymaster F.F. White
Quartermaster J. Pullen
Sergeant-Major F. Gapp

56

CAPTAIN R. YOUNGHUSBAND,
1ST/24TH FOOT

LIEUTENANT C.W. CAVAYE,
1ST/24TH FOOT

LIEUTENANT J.P. DALY,
1ST/24TH FOOT

LIEUTENANT
G.F.J. HODSON,
1ST/24TH FOOT

Quartermaster-Sergeant T. Leitch

Sergeant Instructor of Musketry G. Chambers

Armourer Sergeant H. Hayward

Pay Sergeant G. Mead

Drum-Major R. Taylor

Orderly Room Clerk G. Fitzgerald

Sergeant Cook A. Field

Sergeant Tailor J. Smedley

Canteen Steward W.P. Seaton

Colour-Sergeants: J.G. Ballard; T.P. Brown; W. Edwards; W. Whitfield; F.H. Wolfe

Sergeants: P. Ainsworth; G. Bennett; D. Bradley; J. Clarkson; W. Coholan; T. Cooper; J. Edwards; T. Fay; J. Fowden; E. Giles; J. Greatorex; C. Heppenstall; M. Hornibrook; W. Parsons; A. Piall; J. Reardon; J. Smith; G. Upton

Band Sergeant D. Gamble

Lance-Sergeant J. Milner

Corporals: N. Ball; P. Bell; J. Bellhouse; A.C. Board; R.S. Davies; E.R. Everett; J. Franks; J. Knight; J. Lawler; P. Markham; M. Miller; J. Rowden; J. Tarbuck; R. Williams

Pioneer Corporal H. Richardson

Drummers: W.H. Adams; C. Andrews; G. Dibden, J.F. Orlopp; C. Osmond; T. Perkins; T. Reardon; M. Stansfield; J. Thompson; D. Trottman; A. Wolfendale; J. Wolfendale

Privates: R. Abbott; T. Allingham; E. Amos; A. Atkins; J. Bailey; E. Baker; (466) J. Barry; (727) J. Barry; E. Barsley; J. Bartles; C. Bastard; R. Beadon; J. Benham; A. Bennett; R. Bennett; R. Benson; N. Betterton; J. Birch; J. Bishop; R. Blackhurst; J. Blower; F. Bodman; S. Boulton; J. Boylan; J. Bray; J. Breese; J.W. Brew; J. Broderick; J. Brown; W. Brown; F. Bugby; J. Bull; T. Burke; (176) W. Burke; (886) W. Burke; W. Burns; T. Busby; W.J. Butler; J. Cahill; J. Camp; M. Campbell; J. Cantillon; W.H. Carpenter; P. Carrol; J. Casey; E. Ceiley; W. Chadwick; W. Chalmers; J. Chatterton; W. Chepman; J. Christian; A. Clarke; M. Clarke; W.H. Clements; W. Clutterbuck; A. Cole; J. Coleman; D. Collins; T. Collins; T. Colston; G. Conboye; C. Connolly; J. Connolly; S. Connors; J. Cook; H. Cooper; R. Coughlan; J. Cox; T. Cox; M. Cullen; J. Cullenan; W. Davies; A. Davis; E. Davis; M. Diggle; T. Diggle; J. Dobbin; W. Dobbs; C. Donohoe; M. Doran; J. Dorman; P. Dowde; W.R. Dredge; T. Duck; G. Duckworth; J. Duffy; E.

Dugmore; F. Dunn; J. Dyer; J. Edwards; W.J. Edwards; T. Egan; W. Egan; W. Elderington; G. Elderton; O. Ellis; H. Ellison; J. Ellsmore; D. Evans; J.W. Evans; T. Evry; J. Faircloth; W. Farmer; G.H. Fay; M. Ferris; T. Fitzgerald; E. Flint; W. Flood; J. Fortune; W. Freeman; T. Gilder; J. Gillan; C. Gingell; G. Glass; A. Goatham; C. Goddard; G. Goodchild; T. Goss; W. Green; W. Gregg; W. Gregson; G. Griffiths; G. Hadden; I. Hale; J. Hall; J. Hannaford; T. Harkin; J. Harman; D. Harney; D. Harrington; T.H. Harris; W. Harris; W. Hayden; J. Haynes; J. Hedges; C. Hemmings; J. Hewitt; J. Hibbard; W.H. Hicken; T. Hicks; T.H. Higgins; J. Hind; J. Hitchen; W. Holden; J. Holland; D. Horgan; J. Horn; C. Hornbuckle; E. Hughes; (237) J. Hughes; (404) J. Hughes; O. Hughes; T. Hughes; A. Iggulden; F.G. Ilsley; E. Ivatts; (1083) W. Jenkins; (1767) W. Jenkins; G. Johnson; H. Johnson; J. Johnson; W. Johnson; G. Johnston; (663) J. Johnston; (381) J. Johnston; A. Johnstone; E. Jones; (360) J. Jones; (428) J. Jones; T. Jones; (341) W. Jones; (1682) W. Jones; J. Keane; J. Keegan; A. Kelly; F. Kelly; (520) J. Kelly; (789) J. Kelly; N. Kempsell; J. Kempster; J. Knight; J. Lamb; T. Lambert; J. Lawrence; R. Leach; T. Leaver; J. Lee; H. Lewis; R. Lewis; J. Ling; J. Linnane; S. Lippett; G. Lisbeck; G. Lloyd; W. Lockett; C. Lovell; C.S. Lowe; R. Lowe; J. Lycett; J. Lyons; M. McDonald; M. McFarlane; J. McHale; H.A. Mack; J.J. Mackenzie; G.R. Maer; M. Maloney; W. Mann; L. Marley; C. Marney; D. Martin; J.H. Meredith; C. Millen; P. Miller; R. Moore; J. Morgan; W. Morgan; G. Morris; R. Morse; J. Murphy; P. Murphy; J. Murray; P. Nash; A. Newberry; T. Newberry; W. Nicholas; W.E. Nye; W. Oakley; G. Odey; J. Ogden; J. Padmore; T. Painter; R. Parry; H.H. Patterson; J. Peters; (845) J.N. Phillips; (237) J. Phillips; J.R. Pickard; S. Plant; J. Plunkett; A. Pollen; W. Pope; U. Pottow; H. Powell; J. Proctor; G. Prosser; J. Prosser; (182) W. Pugh; (856) W. Pugh; J. Quirk; E. Remington; W.H. Retford; G. Richards; M. Richardson; J. Rigney; J. Rittman; W. Roberts; H. Rodgers; P. Roubrey; H. Rowman; W. Rule; F. Russell; T. Rutter; J. Ryan; G. Salter; F. Sarney; H. Sears; W. Sellwood; F. Sharp; R. Shaw; D. Shea; H. Sheater; J. Shrimpton; R. Silcock; W. Skelton; (506) C. Smith; (1867) C. Smith; E. Smith; G. Smith; J. Smith; T. Speed; H. Stevens; W. Stevens; E. Strange; J. Sullivan; P. Sullivan; P. Sutton; R. Swoffer; R. Tate; E. Taylor; J. Terry; W. Theobald; (636) J. Thomas; (765) J.B. Thomas; T. Thornett; C. Throssell; H. Tillison; T. Tinnery; G. Todd; J.

Townsend; E. Trowell; J. Tullett; G. Vines; (925) E. Walker; (444) E. Walker; (285) T. Walsh; (493) T. Walsh; W. Walsh; W. Walton; J. Warner; W.H. Watkins; J. Watley; H. Watts; T. Webb; H. Wetherhead; J. Whelan; T. Whelan; E. Whybrow; A. Wilkinson; F. Wilks; (455) E. Williams; (778) E. Williams; (545) J. Williams; (582) J. Williams; (868) J. Williams; M. Williams; (534) T. Williams; (624) T. Williams; W.E. Williams; J. Wilson; S. Wilson; W. Wisher; J. Wood; J. Woolley; E. Worthington; R. Wright; T. Young
Boys: T.J. Harrington; R. Richards

LIEUTENANT
C.D'A. POPE,
2ND/24TH FOOT

2nd Battalion 24th (2nd Warwickshires) Regiment of Foot
Lieutenants: C.D'A. Pope; F. Godwin-Austen; H.J. Dyer
Sub-Lieutenant T.L.G. Griffith
Quartermaster E. Bloomfield
Bandmaster H.T. Bullard
Quartermaster-Sergeant G.H. Davis
Sergeants: H. Carse; C. Chew; J. Lines; W.J.G. Reeves; J. Ross; W. Shaw; G. Wilkins
Lance-Sergeants: J. Haigh; J. McCaffery

61

LIEUTENANT
H.J. DYER,
2ND/24TH FOOT

SUB-LIEUTENANT
T.L.G. GRIFFITH,
2ND/24TH FOOT

Corporals: W. Greenhill; J. Henshaw; J.M. Low; H. Mortlock; G. Sims; G. Thompson
Lance-Corporal J. Elvey
Drummers: J. Anderson; J. Holmes
Privates: J. Allen; J.W. Barton; S. Beavan; T. Bennett; H. Bishop; A. Bray; F. Bridgewater; G.P. Brierly; M. Broderick; W. Bryant; R. Buckley; T. Bull; E.A. Byard; (721) J. Byrne; (1671) J. Byrne; T. Carroll; W. Charles; F. Cherry; M. Cleary; T. Cornish; G. Davies; J.J. Davies; D. Davis; (894) J. Davis; (121) J. Davis; M. Donegan; J. Dowle; J. Earish; E. Edwards; J. Edwards; R. Emerson; J. Evans; A. Farr; T. Finn; G. Fitton; D. Flyn; J. Flyn; M. Fortune; T. Fox; J. Fry; W. Gee; G. Ghost; W. Griffiths, VC; J. Gurney; S. Hacker; B. Hall; C. Hall; J. Hall; W. Hall; L. Hankin; W. Hawkins; J. Healey; J.E. Hill; R.H. Hopkins; G. Horrocks; R. Howells; G. Hudson; F. Hughes; J. Hunt; W. Jenkins; W. Johnstone; A. Jones; E. Jones; J. Jones; (976) T. Jones; (1382) T. Jones; (1511) T. Jones; W. Jones; J. Kelly; T. Kennedy; J. King; B. Latham; E. Lewis; J. Lewis; J. Llewellyn; C. Long; T. Lynch; P. McCaffery; J. McCormack; S. McCracken; G. McDoon; J. McGuire; J. Machin; J. Mack; E. Malley; J. Marsh; E. Martingale; M. Mockler; T. Montgomery; F. Moore; J. Morgan; A. Morris; J. Morrisey; P. Mulroy; J. Murphy; T. Neagle; R. Nobes; T. O'Keefe; H. Perkins; D. Phillips; S. Poole; S. Popple; H. Price; J. Price; D. Pritchard; T. Quilford; J. Quinn; W. Rees; W. Rice; J. Roche; M. Roche; T. Saunders; J. Scott; J. Shean; S. Sherwood; W. Shuttleworth; H. Slade; C.M. Smith; D. Smith; F. Smith; H. Smith; J. Smith; P. Smith; R. Smith; R. Stephens; W. Terrett; D. Thomas; G. Thompson; R. Treverton; T. Vedler; S. Walker; E. Waters; W. Waterhouse; J. Watkins; J. White; T. White; A. Wightman; (463) E. Williams; (1470) E. Williams; (1023) E. Williams; G. Williams; T. Williams; G. Wood; J. Wright; E. Young
Boys: D. Gordon; J.S. McEwan

90th (Perthshire Volunteers) Light Infantry
Privates: G. Broadhurst; H. Edwards; W. Healey; D. Pattrick; T. Walsh; C. Wickham

Army Hospital Corps
Lieutenant of Orderlies A.W. Hall
Corporal J. Lee

Privates: G. Baker; A. Cain; A. Cremer; J. Deane; J. Gillman; J. Hogan; J. Hughes; H.W. Lewis; G.G. Munn

Army Service Corps
Corporal J.J. Pritchard
Privates: F.J. Coles; A. Jacques

1st Squadron Mounted Infantry
(Listed by parent units)

6th Dragoon Guards
Private J. McStravick

9th Lancers
Farrier H. Sampson

2nd Battalion 3rd (East Kent) Regiment of Foot ('The Buffs')
Privates: J. Shaw and G. Wheatley

1st Battalion 24th (2nd Warwickshires) Regiment of Foot
Private E. Turner

80th (The Staffordshire Volunteers) Regiment of Foot
Sergeant W. Johnson
Privates: J. Chesterton; E. Holman; W. McDonald; W. Seymour; J. Whitehouse

Natal Mounted Police
Corporal M. Lally
Lance-Corporal H.M. Campbell
Troopers: G.H. Banger; H. Berry; E. Blakeman; H.I. Capps; J. Clarke; S. Daniels; C.T. Dorey; J. Eason; W. Fletcher; H.C. Lloyd; T. McRae; C.H. Meares; H. Neil; A. Parsons; H.T. Pearce; J. Pleydell; A.F. Pollard; F. Secretan; J.W.M. Siddall; W.E. Stimson; S.C. Thicke; C. White; H. Winkles

Natal Carbineers
Lieutenant F.J.D Scott
Quartermaster W. London
Sergeant J.C. Bullock
Troopers: J.A. Blaikie; G. Borain; C.G.S. Christian; H.W. Davis; J. Deane; H. Dickinson; C. Haldane; W. Hawkins; C. Hayhow; F. Jackson; R. Jackson; J. Lumley; G.T. Macleroy; W. Mendenhall; M. Moodie; J. Ross; W. Swift; E. Tarbarton; J. Whitelaw

LIEUTENANT
F.J.D. SCOTT,
NATAL CARBINEERS

TROOPER
J.A. BLAIKIE,
NATAL CARBINEERS

65

Newcastle Mounted Rifles
Captain C.R. Bradstreet
Quartermaster G.E. Hitchcock
Sergeant-Major A. Swan
Troopers: J.W. Barnes; J. Dinkelman; C. Greenback; A. McAllister

Buffalo Border Guard
Troopers: G. Eary; J. Gutridge; Wehr

1st Battalion, 3rd Regiment, Natal Native Contingent
Captains: R. Krohn; J.F. Lonsdale

CAPTAIN
C.R. BRADSTREET,
NEWCASTLE MOUNTED
RIFLES

Lieutenants: A. Avery; F. Holcraft; C. Jameson
Surgeon F.W. Buée
Quartermaster J.R. McCormack
Interpreter S. Grant
Conductors: J.P.K. Archbell; T.G. Doyle; L.P. Du Bois; Le Roue;
    Nolan
Hospital Sergeant Cane
Sergeants: H. Atkins; G. Bryant; H. Church; J. Cole; J. Connock;
    Donnell; W. Golding; W. Humphries; W. McCarty; C. Patterson;
    W. Russell; J. Walsh

CAPTAIN
J.F. LONSDALE,
1ST/3RD NNC

QUARTERMASTER
J.R. MCCORMACK,
1ST/3RD NNC

Corporals: J. Balmore; Davidson; J. Dupreez; D. O'Connell; M. O'Neil; R. Palmer; J. Pearson; W. Price; J. Quinn; F. Sibley; W. Willey

2nd Battalion, 3rd Regiment, Natal Native Contingent
Captains: A.J. Barry; C.A. Erskine; O.E. Murray
Lieutenants: A. Gibson; R.A. Pritchard; H.O. Rivers; Hon. S.W.P. Vereker, L.D. Young
Quartermaster A.P. Chambers
Quartermaster-Sergeant A. Farr

LIEUTENANT THE HON.
S.W.P. VEREKER,
2ND/3RD NNC

Sergeants: J. Allen; W. Brebner; A. Broderick; M. Broderick; G. Elverson; W. Hamilton; T. Kemp; G. Moore; G.G. Mowbray; W. Murray; S. Phillips; L. Schaap
Corporals: W. Allen; J. Caufield; D. Delaharpe; D. de Villiers; W. Green; T. Harrington; W. Laughlin; T. Pitzer; L. Schneither; N. Stapleton; H. Sturk; R. Styles; J. Walker; E. Welsh; J. Willis

WOUNDED IN ACTION (EUROPEAN)
1st Battalion, 1st Regiment, Natal Native Contingent
Lieutenant W.B. Erskine, assegai wound to thigh

Natal Native Horse
Combined casualties of Sikali's Horse: 27 men
Edendale Troop: two men

Natal Native Contingent
Combined total of casualties from all units engaged: 442 men

WOUNDED IN ACTION (NATIVE FORCES)
Natal Native Horse
Combined casualties of Sikali's Horse: Six men
(Details of wounds unknown to this compiler)

Natal Native Contingent
Combined total of casualties from all units engaged: Ten men
(Details of wounds unknown to this compiler)

Zulu Casualties

Approximately 1,500 men killed or died of wounds

The European Survivors of Isandlwana

NO. 2 COLUMN
Staff: Lieutenant W.F.D. Cochrane, 32nd (Cornwall) Light Infantry;
  Conductor Hamer, locally recruited Transport Department
Rocket Battery: Acting Bombardier G. Goff, 'N' Battery, 5th Brigade, Royal Artillery
Privates: H. Grant; D. Johnson; J. Trainer, 1st Battalion, 24th (2nd
  Warwickshires) Regiment of Foot

Natal Native Horse
Captain W. Barton
Lieutenants: C. Raw; R.W. Vause; A.F. Henderson; H.D. Davis

1st Battalion, 1st Regiment, Natal Native Contingent
Captains: C. Nourse; D.M. Smythe; W.H. Stafford
Lieutenant W.B. Erskine
Sergeant-Major T. Sharp

NO. 3 COLUMN
Staff: Captains: A.C. Gardner, 14th (King's) Hussars; E. Essex, 75th

(Stirlingshire) Regiment of Foot; Lieutenant H.L. Smith-Dorrien, 95th (Derbyshire) Regiment of Foot; Mr J.A. Brickhill, interpreter; Private J. Williams, 1st Battalion, 24th (2nd Warwickshires) Regiment of Foot

'N' Battery, 5th Brigade, Royal Artillery
Lieutenant H.T. Curling
Sergeant J. Costellow, Trumpeter N. Martin
Shoeing-Smiths: J. Steer; G. Townsend; Gunner W. Green
Drivers: J. Baggeley; J. Burchell; E. Price; E. Tucker

1st Battalion, 24th (2nd Warwickshires) Regiment of Foot
Privates: J. Bickley; E. Wilson

1st Squadron Mounted Infantry
(Listed by parent units)

2nd Battalion, 3rd (East Kent) Regiment of Foot ('The Buffs')
Sergeant P. Naughton
Private E. Evans

1st Battalion, 13th (Somerset) Light Infantry
Private D. Whelan

1st Battalion, 24th (2nd Warwickshires) Regiment of Foot
Privates: H. Davis; J. McCan; W. Parry; J. Power

80th (The Staffordshire Volunteers) Regiment of Foot
Privates: S. Wassall, vc; T. Westwood

Natal Mounted Police
Lance-Corporal R.N. Eaton
Trumpeter R. Stevens
Troopers: G. Collier; D. Doig; W.V. Dorehill; W. Hayes; R. Kincaid; R.J. Shannon; C.M.F. Sparks

Natal Carbineers
Troopers: W. Barker; W. Edwards; C. Fletcher; W. Grainger; A. Muirhead; W. Sibthorpe; W. Tarboton

Newcastle Mounted Rifles
Trumpeter Horne
Troopers: Berning; Brown; Burne; D. Moodie; Parsons; Welsh

Buffalo Border Guard
Quartermaster D. McPhail

Quartermaster-Sergeant Adams
Troopers: Adams; Lennox; Stretch

1st Battalion, 3rd Regiment, Natal Native Contingent
Lieutenants: J. Adendorff; T. Vaines

2nd Battalion, 3rd Regiment, Natal Native Contingent
Lieutenant and Adjutant W.C.R. Higginson
Lieutenant H. Fairclough
Sergeant-Major Williams

No. 1 Company, Natal Native Pioneers
Lieutenant G.F. Andrews

Locally Recruited Transport Department
Conductor Foley

Unit Not Determined
R.J. Hall
T. Hill
Stevenson

HONOURS AND AWARDS

The Victoria Cross
Private S. WASSALL, 80th Foot
The London Gazette
17th June 1879
For his gallant conduct in having, at the imminent risk of his own life, saved that of Private Westwood of the same regiment.

On the 22nd January 1879, when the Camp at Isandhlwana [sic] was taken by the enemy, Private Wassall retreated towards the Buffalo River, in which he saw a comrade struggling and apparently drowning. He rode to the bank, dismounted, leaving his horse on the Zulu side, rescued the man from the stream and again mounted his horse, dragging Private Westwood across the river under a heavy shower of bullets.

*

Lieutenants T. MEVILL and N.J.A. COGHILL, 1st/24th Foot
Supplement to The London Gazette – 2nd May 1879
MEMORANDUM
Lieutenant Melville [sic] of the 1st Battalion 24th Foot, on account of

LIEUTENANT
T. MELVILL, VC,
1ST/24TH FOOT

LIEUTENANT
N.J.A. COGHILL, VC,
1ST/24TH FOOT

the gallant efforts made by him to save the Queen's Colour of his Regiment after the disaster at Isandlwanha [sic], and also Lieutenant Coghill, 1st Battalion, 24th Foot, on account of his heroic conduct in endeavouring to save his brother officer's life, would have been recommended to Her Majesty for the Victoria Cross had they survived.

[In 1879 there was no provision for the posthumous award of the Victoria Cross. It was not until 1907 that the families of these two officers received the decoration.]

V

The Defence of the Mission Station, Rorke's Drift, Natal Wednesday, 22nd–Thursday, 23rd January 1879

'Let us go and have a fight at Jim's'
— *A Zulu Warrior*

FOLLOWING THE departure of Durnford's troops to join the force at Isandlwana, the depot at Rorke's Drift returned to normality. The mission station of Otto Witt, the resident missionary, had been requisitioned as a storehouse and hospital, known colloquially to the Zulu as kwa Jimu – Jim's Place – after a trader, James Rorke, who had resided there from 1849 until his death in 1875. The station was dominated by a hill named by Witt, 'Oskarberg' but known to the Zulu as 'Shiyane'. Surgeon J.H. Reynolds of the Army Medical Department, assisted by three other ranks of the Army Hospital Corps, made the rounds of the thirty-six sick and wounded men. Lieutenant J.R.M. Chard, Royal Engineers, obtained permission from Brevet Major H. Spalding, 104th Foot, the Deputy Assistant Quartermaster General and officer commanding the depot, to ride to Isandlwana early on the morning of 22nd January, to clarify his orders as to what duties he should perform regarding entrenching the Natal bank of the Drift.

The post was protected by 'B' Company, 2nd Battalion of the 24th Regiment of Foot, commanded by Lieutenant G. Bromhead. The company should have been reinforced two days previously by Companies 'D' and 'G' of the 1st/24th stationed at Helpmakaar. Also forming part of the guard was a

company of the 2nd/3rd Natal Native Contingent, commanded by Captain W. Stevenson. The responsibility for stores fell
to Assistant Commissary W.A. Dunne, assisted by two volunteers, Acting Assistant Commissary J.L. Dalton and Acting
Storekeeper L.A. Byrne, and also Second Corporal F.
Attwood, Army Service Corps.

Later that morning, Chard returned from Isandlwana with
his position verified: he was to remain and superintend the
ponts at Rorke's Drift. He acquainted Spalding with intelligence he had gained whilst at Isandlwana concerning a large
body of Zulus that had been seen moving along the Nquthu
plateau. This prompted Spalding to decide to accelerate the
reinforcement from Helpmekaar. Spalding consulted his
Army List to ascertain who was the senior of the two lieutenants, and the command devolved to Chard. Spalding then
set out towards Helpmekaar.

Chard retired for lunch to his tent by the Drift, some half a
mile from the mission station. The muffled sound of gunfire
had been heard from the direction of Isandlwana, but had
caused no undue alarm. At 3.15 p.m., however, Chard was
writing a letter home when his attention was drawn to two
horsemen frantically hailing the pont guard from the Zulu
bank. After being ferried across Lieutenants Adendorff and
Vaines of the NNC, two of the few survivors from Isandlwana,
told Chard of the disaster which had befallen the force there.
Chard promptly deployed Sergeant F. Millne, 2nd/3rd Regiment of Foot, and six men of the 24th, including Lance
Sergeant T. Williams, 2nd/24th, on the high ground above the
ponts, with a commanding field of fire.

Vaines then rode on to Helpmekaar to spread the word of
the disaster at Isandlwana.

Chard hurried back to the mission station, after a summons
from Bromhead. On his arrival he found preparations for a
defence had already begun under the direction of Dalton, as
the post had been alerted by other survivors. Dalton, a former
senior non-commissioned officer, proved invaluable. Utilising
the only resources that were available, he supervised the

OTTO WITT

LIEUTENANT
J.R.M. CHARD, RE

LIEUTENANT
G. BROMHEAD,
2ND/24TH FOOT

ASSISTANT COMMISSARY
W.A. DUNNE,
COMMISSARIAT AND
TRANSPORT DEPARTMENT

construction of a barricade from mealie bags and biscuit boxes. Chard then returned to the small detachment by the Buffalo where the civilian ferryman, Mr Daniells, and Sergeant Millne offered to moor the ponts midstream and, with the six men of the pont guard, to defend them in an effort to gain valuable time for Chard. Although heartened by the offer, Chard declined it; he was going to need every man he had for the defence.

At about 3.30 p.m. Lieutenant A.F. Henderson arrived with some one hundred men of the Hlubi and Edendale Troops, Natal Native Horse. Chard had them thrown out in a mounted screen, observing the Drift and the reverse slope of the Oskarberg. Several more survivors from Isandlwana arrived and attempted to impress on the garrison the futility of a defence, but Chard's resolve could not be altered. It was fight not flight. The survivors, however, having seen the horror of Isandlwana, and believing the same fate would surely befall Rorke's Drift, continued their flight. Witt, too, rode off to Umsinga, where he had sent his family for safety, taking with him Lieutenant T. Purvis, who had been recovering in the hospital from a wound received at Sihayo's Kraal.

At about 4.20 p.m. sporadic gunfire was heard behind the Oskarberg, and the Natal Native Horse galloped past the mission station in the direction of Helpmekaar. Lieutenant Henderson, pausing only to report that his troops refused to obey orders, took off in pursuit of them. Then Stevenson's disheartened company of Natal Native Contingent also decamped, enraging some members of the garrison who fired on the fleeing NNC, one of the bullets finding its mark in the back of Corporal W. Anderson, a white non-commissioned officer.

Private F. Hitch, perched on the hospital roof, then yelled a warning. About 500 Zulus were advancing towards the south wall. As the Zulus came within 500 yards of the south wall the defenders opened fire – erratically at first, then more steadily. A mounted induna was brought down by Private J. Dunbar. Despite sustaining heavy casualties the Zulus advanced to within fifty yards of the rear of the hospital, only to be checked

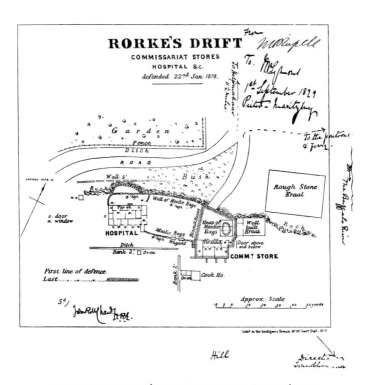

LIEUTENANT J.R.M. CHARD'S PLAN OF THE POSITION AT RORKE'S DRIFT

A VIEW OF THE MISSION STATION AT RORKE'S DRIFT BEFORE THE ATTACK.
THIS TRANQUIL SCENE WOULD BE SHATTERED BY THE ONSLAUGHT OF SOME FOUR THOUSAND
ZULU WARRIORS INTENT ON DESTROYING THE SMALL GARRISON.

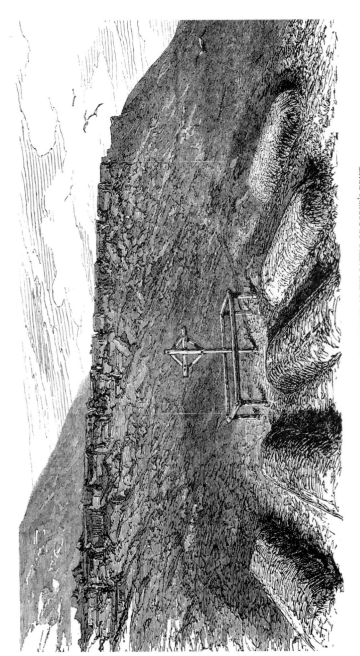

THE TEMPORARY RESTING PLACE FOR THE FALLEN OF THE BATTLE OF RORKE'S DRIFT.
THE CRUDE WOODEN CROSS WAS SUBSEQUENTLY REPLACED BY A MEMORIAL OBELISK.

in a crossfire between the south wall, the rear wall of the hospital and the Commissariat store. There they sought cover by the cook house ovens to avoid the murderous hail of fire from the barricade. A large body of Zulus, commanded by Prince Dabulamanzi kaMpande, swept past the hospital, some assailing its south-west apex. The Zulus who had taken cover by the cook house began firing at the barricade, and Zulu riflemen positioned on the Oskarberg added to the fire. The barricade in front of the hospital came under heavy assault and

PRINCE DABULAMANZI
KAMPANDE

a desperate fight ensued – the defenders locked in struggle with the Zulus, assegai traded with bayonet. The defenders were driven back across the frontage of the hospital, and the Zulus poured over the barricade. Only a timely bayonet charge led by Bromhead repulsed the Zulus, sending them scurrying back over the defences.

The Zulus now vented their anger on the side door of the hospital. Their furious assault was met with stubborn defence by Privates John Williams and Joseph Williams of the 2nd/

24th and W. Horrigan of the 1st/24th, a hospital patient who had taken up a rifle and joined the defence. Also present in the room but unable to help because of their ailments were three other patients, Private W. Beckett, 1st/24th and Privates R. Adams and G. Hayden, 2nd/24th.

Their ammunition expended, Joseph Williams held the doorway with the point of his bayonet whilst John Williams smashed a hole in the partition wall. To add to the horror the thatched roof of the hospital was now ablaze. Joseph Williams was seized, dragged through the doorway and killed outside. Adams and Hayden died in their beds, helpless under a flurry of assegais. John Williams, assisted by Horrigan, succeeded in escaping with Beckett into the adjoining room. By this time the Zulus had forced the defenders at the front of the hospital to retire, and were now entering from the verandah. Horrigan met his end in that room, whilst Williams managed to reach the safety of another room with eight patients and now defended by Privates J. Waters, 1st/24th and A.H. Hook, 2nd/24th. Hook had been forced to abandon his original position in the south-west corner of the hospital, where a wounded native Private of the Natal Native Contingent had perished. Waters had sustained a gun shot wound to his arm and shoulder, which Hook dressed in an effort to staunch the bleeding. Williams quickly grasped the situation and began knocking a hole in the partition wall. Hook took up a position in the doorway to fend off the Zulu assault, and whilst doing so he sustained a slight assegai wound to his scalp.

Williams breached the wall, and the sick passed through into the next room. Again Williams breached the wall, whilst Hook covered the line of retreat. Waters and Beckett could go no further and whilst the other patients evacuated they chose to hide in a cupboard in an effort to evade the Zulus. Hook, Williams and the patients reached a room in the south-east corner and found it defended by Privates R. Jones and W. Jones who had in their charge seven sick men, of whom only one, Trooper H. Lugg of the Natal Mounted Police, had been able enough to assist in the defence. The helpless hospital patients were lowered from a window into the arms of Corporal W.W. Allan and Private F. Hitch. Whilst Privates R. Jones and W. Jones held the door (in the process of which R. Jones was slightly injured by thrusting assegais) the last room was evacuated with one exception: Sergeant R. Maxfield, 2nd/24th was delirious and unable to be rescued. With much regret he was left to his fate.

The choking smoke and intense heat forced Beckett and Waters to leave the dubious safety of their cupboard. Fleeing

ACTING ASSISTANT
COMMISSARY J.L. DALTON,
COMMISSARIAT AND
TRANSPORT DEPARTMENT

through the rear door of the hospital, Beckett ran into a group of warriors, one of whom thrust at him with his assegai, the wound penetrating his abdomen. Beckett fell mortally wounded but Waters somehow managed to evade the Zulus and hid.

It was not easy either for those who had escaped through the hospital window. They had to cross a bullet swept compound to reach a newly established inner line of defence. Trooper R. Green of the Natal Mounted Police was struck in the side by a spent round, but with assistance managed to reach the barricade. A fellow policeman, Trooper S. Hunter, was not so lucky. Bewildered because of his illness he was assegaied, losing his life within sight of safety. The remainder of the evacuees and their escort reached the safety of the barricade of biscuit boxes. Dalton, the architect of the defences, fell wounded, shot through the upper body. The entire perimeter of the defences was now engaged, the scene illuminated by the burning hospital.

The ferocity of the Zulu attacks dwindled after about 10 p.m. to small rushes. The Zulu fire also slackened but persisted until about 4 a.m. Dawn broke over the mission station and Chard set about strengthening the barricade. A number of Zulus were seen gathering on the Oskarberg but no attack was forthcoming. Then at about 8 a.m. they abandoned their position on the hill and made off. At 8.15 a.m. Lieutenant-Colonel (local rank) J.C. Russell, 12th (Prince of Wales' Royal) Lancers, leaading an advanced guard of Mounted Infantry from Chelmsford's retreating column, relieved the mission station. The battle was over.

Composition of the British Force

Lieutenant J.R.M. Chard, 5th (Field) Company, Royal Engineers, commanding:
Staff: Sergeant G.W. Mabin

'N' Battery, 5th Brigade, Royal Artillery
Bombardier T. Lewis
Wheeler J. Cantwell
Gunners: A. Evans and A. Howard

5th (Field) Company, Royal Engineers
Driver E. Robson

2nd Battalion, 3rd (East Kent) Regiment of Foot ('The Buffs')
Sergeant F. Millne

1st Battalion, 24th (2nd Warwickshires) Regiment of Foot
Sergeant E. Wilson

Privates: W. Beckett; P. Desmond; W. Horrigan; J. Jenkins; E. Nicholas; T. Payton; W. Roy; H. Turner; J. Waters

2nd Battalion, 24th (2nd Warwickshires) Regiment of Foot
Lieutenant G. Bromhead
Colour-Sergeant F.E. Bourne
Sergeants: H. Gallagher; R. Maxfield; G. Smith; J. Windridge
Lance-Sergeants: J. Taylor; T. Williams
Corporals: W.W. Allan; G. French; J. Key; (1112) J. Lyons; A. Saxty
Lance-Corporals: W. Bessell; W. Halley
Drummers: P. Galgey; P. Hayes; J. Keefe; J. Meehan
Privates: R. Adams; J. Ashton; T. Barry; W. Bennett; J. Bly; J. Bromwich; T. Buckley; T. Burke; J. Bushe; W.H. Camp; T. Chester; J. Chick; T. Clayton; R. Cole; T. Cole; T. Collins; J. Connolly; A. Connors; T. Connors; W. Cooper; G. Davies; W.H. Davis; T. Daw; T. Driscoll; J. Dunbar; G. Edwards; J. Fagan; E. Gee; J. Hagan; J. Harris; G. Hayden; F. Hitch; A.H. Hook; J. Jobbins; E. Jones; R. Jones; W. Jones; P. Judge; P. Kears; M. Kiley; D. Lloyd; T. Lockhart; J. Lodge; T.M. Lynch; (1441) J. Lyons; J. Mauley; J. Marshall; H. Martin; C. Mason; M. Minehan; T. Moffatt; A. Morris; F. Morris; T. Morrison; J. Murphy; W. Neville; R. Norris; W. Osborne; S. Parry; W. Partridge; S. Pitts; T. Robinson; J. Ruck; E. Savage; J. Scanlon; A. Sears; G. Shearman; J. Shergold; J. Smith; T. Stevens; W. Tasker; F. Taylor; T.E. Taylor; J. Thomas; P. Tobin; W.J. Todd; R. Tongue; (1395) J. Williams; (934) J. Williams; (1398) J. Williams; C. Woods

90th (Perthshire Volunteers) Light Infantry
Corporal J. Graham

Commissariat and Transport Department
Assistant Commissary W.A. Dunne
Acting Assistant Commissary J.L. Dalton
Acting Storekeeper L.A. Byrne

Army Service Corps
Second Corporal F. Attwood

Army Medical Department
Surgeon J.H. Reynolds
Mr Pearce (surgeon's servant)

ACTING STOREKEEPER
L.A. BYRNE,
COMMISSARIAT AND
TRANSPORT DEPARTMENT

SURGEON J.H. REYNOLDS,
ARMY MEDICAL DEPARTMENT

Army Hospital Corps
Corporal R. Miller
2nd Corporal M. McMahon
Private T. Luddington

Honorary Chaplain, Weenen Yeomanry
The Rev G. Smith, Vicar of Escourt

Natal Mounted Police
Troopers: R. Green; S. Hunter; H. Lugg

Natal Native Contingent
Lieutenant J. Adendorff
Corporals: M. Doughty; J.H. Mayer; C. Scammel; C.F. Schiess; J.
    Wilson
Native Private (Name Unknown)

Civilian
Mr Daniells (Ferryman)

British and Colonial Casualties

KILLED IN ACTION
1st Battalion, 24th (2nd Warwickshires) Regiment of Foot
Privates: W. Horrigan; J. Jenkins; E. Nicholas

2nd Battalion, 24th (2nd Warwickshires) Regiment of Foot
Sergeant R. Maxfield
Privates: R. Adams; J. Chick; T. Cole; J. Fagan; G. Hayden; J.
    Scanlon; J. Williams

Commissariat and Transport Department
Acting Storekeeper L.A. Byrne

Natal Mounted Police
Trooper S. Hunter

Natal Native Contingent
Native Private (Name Unknown)

WOUNDED IN ACTION
1st Battalion, 24th (2nd Warwickshires) Regiment of Foot
Private W. Beckett, mortally wounded. Died of wounds 23rd January 1879

Private P. Desmond, slightly wounded
Private J. Waters, severely wounded

2nd Battalion, 24th (2nd Warwickshires) Regiment of Foot
Lance-Sergeant T. Williams, mortally wounded. Died of wounds,
    25th January 1879
Corporal W.W. Allan, severely wounded
Corporal J. Lyons, dangerously wounded
Drummer J. Keefe, slightly wounded
Private J. Bushe, slightly wounded
Private F. Hitch, dangerously wounded
Private A.H. Hook, slightly wounded
Private R. Jones, slightly wounded
Private J. Smith, slightly wounded
Private W. Tasker, slightly wounded

Commissariat and Transport Department
Acting Assistant Commissary J.L. Dalton, severely wounded

Natal Mounted Police
Trooper R. Green, slightly wounded

Natal Native Contingent
Corporal C. Scammell, dangerously wounded
Corporal C.F. Schiess, slightly wounded

KILLED
Corporal W. Anderson (By British fire)

Zulu Casualties

500 killed or mortally wounded. At least two prisoners taken alive
    who were subsequently hanged.

HONOURS AND AWARDS

The Victoria Cross
Lieutenant J.R.M. CHARD, Royal Engineers and Lieutenant G.
    BROMHEAD, 2nd/24th Regiment of Foot
Supplement to The London Gazette
2nd May 1879
For their gallant conduct at the defence of Rorke's Drift on the

occasion of the attack by the Zulus on the 22nd and 23rd January 1879.

The Lieutenant-General commanding the troops reports that, had it not been for the fine example and excellent behaviour of these two Officers under the most trying circumstances, the defence of Rorke's Drift post would not have been conducted with that intelligence and tenacity which so essentially characterised it.

The Lieutenant-General adds, that its success must, in a great degree, be attributable to the two young Officers who exercised the Chief Command on the occasion in question.

*

Private John WILLIAMS, 2nd/24th Regiment of Foot
Supplement to The London Gazette
2nd May 1879
Private John Williams was posted with Private Joseph Williams and Private William Horrigan, 1st Battalion, 24th Regiment, in a distant room of the hospital, which they held for more than an hour, so long as they had a round of ammunition left: as communication was for the time cut off, the Zulus were enabled to advance and burst open the door; they dragged out Private Joseph Williams and two of the patients, and assagaied them. Whilst the Zulus were occupied with the slaughter of these men a lull took place, during which Private John Williams, who, with two patients, were the only men now left alive in this ward, succeeded in knocking a hole in the partition and in taking the two patients into the next ward, where he found Private Hook.

*

Private Henry [sic] HOOK, 2nd/24th Regiment of Foot
Supplement to The London Gazette
2nd May 1879
These two men together, one man working whilst the other fought and held the enemy at bay with his bayonet, broke through three more partitions, and were thus enabled to bring eight patients through a small window into the inner line of defence.

*

Private William JONES and Private Robert JONES, 2nd/24th Regiment of Foot
Supplement to The London Gazette
2nd May 1879
In another ward, facing the hill, Private William Jones and Private Robert Jones defended the post to the last, until six out of the seven patients it contained had been removed. The seventh, Sergeant Maxfield, 2nd Battalion, 24th Regiment, was delirious from fever. Although they had previously dressed him, they were unable to induce him to move. When Private Robert Jones returned to en-

CORPORAL W.W. ALLAN, 2ND/24TH FOOT

deavour to carry him away, he found him being stabbed by the Zulus as he lay on his bed.

*

Corporal William ALLEN (sic) and Private Frederick HITCH, 2nd/24th Regiment of Foot
Supplement to The London Gazette
2nd May 1879
It was chiefly due to the courageous conduct of these men that communication with the hospital was kept up at all. Holding

together at all costs a most dangerous post, raked in reverse by the enemy's fire from the hill, they were both severely wounded, but their determined conduct enabled the patients to be withdrawn from the hospital, and when incapacitated by their wounds from fighting, they continued, as soon as their wounds had been dressed, to serve out ammunition to their comrades during the night.

*

Surgeon-Major James Henry REYNOLDS, Army Medical Department (Promoted to Surgeon-Major, 23rd January 1879)
The London Gazette
17th June 1879
For the conspicuous bravery, during the attack at Rorke's Drift on the 22nd and 23rd January 1879, which he exhibited in his constant attention to the wounded under fire, and in his voluntarily conveying ammunition from the store to the defenders of the Hospital, whereby he exposed himself to a cross-fire from the enemy both in going and returning.

*

Acting Assistant Commissary James Langley DALTON, Commissariat and Transport Department
The London Gazette
18th November 1879
For his conspicuous gallantry during the attack on Rorke's Drift Post by the Zulus on the night of the 22nd January 1879, when he actively superintended the work of defence, and was amongst the foremost of those who received the first attack on the corner of the hospital, where the deadliness of his fire did great execution, and the mad rush of the Zulus met its first check, and where by his cool courage he saved the life of a man of the Army Hospital Corps by shooting the Zulu, who, having seized the muzzle of the man's rifle, was in the act of assegaing [sic] him.

This Officer, to whose energy much of the defence of the place was due, was severely wounded during the contest, but still continued to give the same example of cool courage.

*

Corporal (C.F.) Schiess, Natal Native Contingent
The London Gazette
2nd December 1879
For conspicuous gallantry in the defence of Rorke's Drift Post on the night of the 22nd January 1879, when, in spite of his having been wounded in the foot a few days previously, he greatly distinguished himself when the Garrison were repulsing, with the bayonet, a series of desperate assaults made by the Zulus, and displayed great activity and devoted gallantry throughout the defence. On one occasion when the Garrison had retired to the inner line of defence, and the

PRIVATE W. ROY, 1ST/24TH FOOT

Zulus occupied the wall of mealie bags which had been abandoned, he crept along the wall, without any order, to dislodge a Zulu who was shooting better than usual and succeeded in killing him, and two others, before he, the Corporal, returned to the inner defence.

*

The Silver Medal for Distinguished Conduct in the Field

Regiment/Corps	Name	Date of Submission
2nd/24th Foot	Colour-Sergeant F.E. Bourne	28/7/1879

Army Service Corps	Second-Corporal F. Attwood	29/7/1879
1st/24th Foot	Private W. Roy	22/10/1879
Army Hospital Corps	Second-Corporal M. McMahon	15/1/1880 (Award Cancelled)
'N' Battery, 5th Brigade Royal Artillery	Wheeler J. Cantwell	11/2/1880

VI

The Attack at Ntombe Drift
Wednesday, 12th March 1879

'Fire away, boys, death or glory . . .'
— Captain D.B. Moriarty, 80th (Staffordshire
Volunteers) Regiment of Foot

IN THE wake of Isandlwana, Lord Chelmsford was forced to
reappraise his campaign against the Zulus. He had under-
estimated their fighting prowess, and lost the initiative. Until
the arrival of reinforcements, he would have to deploy his
remaining forces appropriately. As a consequence of this,
Brevet Colonel H.E. Wood, VC, absorbed the forces previously
under the command of Colonel H. Rowlands, VC, into his own
command.

Major C. Tucker commanded five companies of the 80th
Foot stationed at Luneburg. The supply line to Luneburg,
stretched 160 miles from Lydenburg, via the townships of
Middleburg and Derby. In late February a supply column of
eighteen wagons filled with ammunition and other provisions
was sent out from Lydenburg without an escort.

On Saturday 1st March, Tucker despatched 'D' Company,
80th Foot commanded by Captain W.T. Anderson, to escort
the convoy on the last leg of its journey, through the country of
the renegade Swazi Prince Mbilini. Mbilini, although a Swazi,
had sworn fidelity to King Cetshwayo, and commanded a
mixed force of Swazis and Zulus. Anderson and his men
crossed the Ntombe River at Myer's Drift and located the
convoy some miles north of the crossing. Its progress had been
impeded by worsening weather conditions.

On Wednesday the 5th however, Anderson and his men were recalled by Tucker to Luneburg since Tucker had received intelligence that Mbilini was planning an assault on Luneburg. Anderson and his party were thus forced to abandon the wagons, with their eleven civilian wagon conductors and thirty native voorloopers to fend for themselves. On Friday, the 7th, as the expected attack had not materialised, Captain D.B. Moriarty, 80th Foot, was ordered to recover the wagons. He was accompanied by Lieutenants A.H. Lindop and H.J. Johnson, 80th Foot, and Dr W.J. Cobbin, a civil surgeon seconded to the Army Medical Department. The escort was found by 103 men of the 80th Foot.

On arrival at the Drift, Moriarty was compelled to pitch his camp on the southern bank of the Ntombe since it was swollen by heavy rains. A raft was contrived using barrels and planks and eventually Moriarty, Johnson, Cobbin and sixty-eight other ranks crossed the river. Lindop remained on the south bank where he set about directing the remaining thirty-five other ranks to improve the crossing point.

Moriarty and his men pressed on and soon found the wagons but on the previous evening Mbilini's men had also found them. They had plundered the supplies and driven off forty-six draught oxen during the absence of a military presence.

Eventually at 2 p.m. on Tuesday, 11th March, Moriarty at last reached the north bank of the Ntombe again. Here he formed the wagons into an inverted V shape, with its base against the river bank. Major Tucker visited the encampment and brought with him Lieutenant H.H. Harward, 80th Foot. By now the incessant rain had ceased, and the level of the Ntombe had fallen. Tucker expressed his anxiety to Moriarty about the defensive position of the laager, but gave no instructions to alter it. Instead he left the laager, taking with him Johnson and Lindop, and returned to Luneburg.

Lieutenant Harward remained with orders to recover some stray livestock. He set out on a reconnaissance accompanied by a small number of other ranks and made contact with a few

A CONVOY UNDER ESCORT BY MEN OF THE 80TH FOOT

THE ATTACK ON THE ENCAMPED CONVOY,
NTOMBE RIVER, WEDNESDAY, 12TH MARCH 1879

armed natives. In the ensuing skirmish at least two natives were killed; Harward succeeded in capturing a few rifles and goats, but failed to locate the stray livestock. He retired to Moriarty's tent to sleep, but Moriarty instructed him to take charge of the section on the southern bank.

Two sentinels were placed on the northern bank and a third on the southern. A heavy mist formed on the Ntombe. At about 4 a.m. the following day, the sentry on the southern bank roused Harward, reporting that he had heard a distant report of a firearm. Harward fell his men in and sent a man across the river to inform Moriarty of the occurrence. Moriarty turned his men out, but he apparently considered it to be a false alarm for he permitted his men to return to their beds. He did, however, caution his sentries to be vigilant.

At about 5 a.m., as the mist began to lift, a volley broke the silence, heralding the attack of about 900 of Mbilini's Swazis and Zulus. Roused from slumber, the men of the 80th attempted to defend themselves. Moriarty tumbled from his tent, sword and revolver in hand and yelled, 'Guards out!' An assegai caught him in his back, but he still managed to shoot dead three Zulus. He was then shot in the chest but as he fell he cried out: 'Fire away, boys, death or glory. I am done!'

Ferocious fighting ensued, but the result was inevitable. Somehow a small number evaded the massacre and fled to the dubious safety of the southern shore, covered by the rifles of Harward's party. A body of Zulus numbering about two hundred swept over the river in an effort to cut any line of retreat open to Harward's men. Those who had been involved in the slaughter of Moriarty's men also turned their attention on Harward's party, and began to stream across the Ntombe.

Harward then made a rash decision. He ordered Sergeant A. Booth, 80th Foot, to fall back on a deserted farmhouse some three miles from the Drift with the remaining troops. Having given these orders, Harward mounted his horse and set off at a gallop towards Luneburg. Booth and his party fought a heroic retreat, engaging the Zulus as they came close. Four men fled the safety of this small knot of men and quickly perished.

Booth continued his fighting retreat and eventually gained the safety of the farmhouse, without further loss.

Harward reached Luneburg at about 6.30 a.m. In a state of anguish he blurted out to Tucker that the camp had fallen to the enemy. Tucker hastily gathered up as many horses and men as he could find and set out for the Ntombe. He also instructed two under-strength companies to follow. The mounted men reached Booth's men and, satisfied as to their safety, pushed on to the Ntombe.

On his arrival at the Ntombe he was greeted by a scene of destruction. The stores had been pillaged, and Moriarty and many of his command had been ritually disembowelled.

Composition of the British Force

Captain D.B. Moriarty, 80th (The Staffordshire Volunteers) Regiment of Foot, *commanding:*

80th (The Staffordshire Volunteers) Regiment of Foot
103 other ranks

Army Medical Department (Seconded)
Dr W.J. Cobbin

Locally Recruited Transport Department
11 men

Native Voorloopers
30 men

British Casualties

KILLED IN ACTION
80th (The Staffordshire Volunteers) Regiment of Foot
Captain D.B. Moriarty
Lance-Sergeants: G. Sansam; H. Johnson
Corporal J. McCoy
Privates: J. Adey; J. Anthony; A. Banks; G. Broughton; J. Brown; H. Brownson; J. Chadwick; J. Christie; A. Day; H. Dutton; W. Findley; W. Fox; E. Gittings; J. Green; G. Haines; H. Hill; T. Hodges; J. Hughes; J. Ingram; H. Jacobs; J. Laffarty; R. Leese; B.

McSherry; H. Meadows; A. Middow; G. Mitchel; R. Moore; W. Moran; H. Night; W. Phipps; F. Ralphs; J. Robinson; H. Ruffle; J. Tibbett; T. Tucker; J. Vernon; J. Weaver

Army Medical Department (Seconded)
Dr W.J. Cobbin

Locally Recruited Transport Department
Conductors: J. Whittington; Campbell

CAPTAIN
D.B. MORIARTY,
80TH FOOT

MISSING IN ACTION (presumed dead)
80th (The Staffordshire Volunteers) Regiment of Foot
Colour Sergeant H. Fredericks
Drummer J. Leather
Privates: J. Banner; J. Dodd; W. Farnell; W. Flyfield; J. Fourneaux; G. Hadley; J. Hart; E. Hawkes; T. Healey; H. Lodge; C. Pritchard; A. Pummell; M. Sheridan; J. Silcock; H. Smith; R. Tomlinson; G. Tucker; H. Woodward

Locally Recruited Transport Department
Conductor Goss

Native Voorloopers
Seven drivers and seven leaders (details unknown)

Zulu/Swazi Casualties

25 dead found at the scene of the action. Two severely wounded men taken prisoner. The official death toll was given as 200 killed, but this appears to be a wild exaggeration.

LIEUTENANT
H.H. HARWARD,
80TH FOOT

Postscript

There was another casualty of the action on the Ntombe, a victim of circumstance.

Lieutenant H.H. Harward was tried by a general court-martial at Fort Napier, Pietermaritzburg, on 20th February 1880. Two charges were brought before the court:

1. Of having misbehaved before the enemy, in shamefully abandoning a party of the regiment under his command when attacked by the enemy, and in riding off at speed from his men.

102

2. Of conduct to the prejudice of good order and military discipline in having, at the place and time mentioned in the first charge, neglected to take proper precautions for the safety of a party of a regiment under his command when attacked.

The court found Harward 'not guilty' on both counts. The findings of the court were submitted for formal approval to Sir Garnet Wolseley. He disapproved of the findings and would not confirm them. However, Harward was released and allowed to return to duty. Wolseley informed the Commander-in-Chief of the British Army, His Royal Highness The Duke of Cambridge, of his concern regarding Harward's actions, concluding in no uncertain terms that Harward had betrayed the trust between an officer and those under his command.

On 13th May 1880 the Duke of Cambridge issued a General Order, which expressed that Wolseley's comments were to be read at the head of every regiment in Her Majesty Queen Victoria's service. Harward was by then no longer in the service of her Majesty: rather than suffering such a public humiliation he resigned his commission on 11th May.

HONOURS AND AWARDS

The Victoria Cross
Colour Sergeant Anthony BOOTH (Promoted to Colour Sergeant, 13th March 1879)
The London Gazette
24th February 1880
For his gallant conduct on the 12th March 1879, during the Zulu attack on the Intombi River, in having, when considerably outnumbered by the enemy, rallied a few men on the south bank of the river, and covered the retreat of fifty soldiers and others for a distance of three miles. The Officer Commanding 80th Regiment reports that, had it not been for the coolness displayed by this Non-commissioned Officer, not one man would have escaped.

VII

The Assault on Hlobane
Friday, 28th March 1879

'Are you doubtful, sir, of our getting up to the top of the mountain?' – Mr L. Lloyd and Lt H. Lysons, 90th (Perthshire Volunteers) Light Infantry

B Y MARCH 1879, Chelmsford's original invasion plans lay in tatters. He had only one cohesive fighting force under his command – No. 4 Column. Chelmsford desperately needed another victory to silence his critics at home. He ordered Brevet Colonel H.E. Wood, VC, to create a diversion in his theatre of operations on 28th March, hoping that this would draw off some of the Zulu forces besieging Pearson at Eshowe, thus enabling a relief of the besieged No. 1 Column. Wood planned to raid the stronghold situated on the plateau at Hlobane Mountain. This stronghold, which had been a menace since the invasion, was held by the abaQulusi, who were of Zulu stock, and Mbilini's men – in all, about 800 warriors. It was Wood's intention to drive off the cattle herds from the mountain and fall back on Khambula, thus, he hoped, forcing an attack on his prepared defences.

Wood planned a two-pronged assault on the mountain: from the east by a detachment commanded by Brevet Lieutenant-Colonel R.H. Buller, 60th Rifles, and from the west by a detachment commanded by Lieutenant-Colonel (local rank) J.C. Russell, 12th Lancers.

At 9 a.m. on Thursday the 27th, Buller's force, comprising a rocket battery, mounted volunteers and a battalion of natives of Wood's Irregulars, left Khambula. Russell's force left at about noon. Comprising a rocket battery, No. 1 Squadron

Mounted Infantry, Natal Native Horse, the Kaffrarian Rifles and a battalion of Wood's Irregulars, it also included 200 followers of Prince Hamu kaNzibe. (Prince Hamu kaNzibe, half brother to King Cetshwayo, had defected to the British cause in early March, bringing with him 700 followers.)

Wood himself left Khambula accompanied by Lieutenant H. Lysons, 90th Light Infantry, orderly officer; Mr L. Lloyd, political assistant and interpreter; Captain the Hon R. Campbell, Coldstream Guards; and a personal escort of eight mounted infantrymen of the 90th Light Infantry and seven mounted 'friendly' Zulus. The two forces halted approximately four miles from their respective objectives and bivouacked for the night.

At 3 a.m. on Friday the 28th, Buller's men commenced their difficult ascent. To add to their problems a storm broke over them. A sense of foreboding must have overwhelmed Wood for when Lloyd and Lysons, eager for the fray, asked him, 'Are you doubtful, sir of our getting to the top of the mountain?' he replied, 'Oh no, we shall get up.' They then enquired 'Then of what are you thinking?' to which he replied 'Well, which of you will be writing to my wife tonight, or about which of you young men I shall be writing to parents or wife?' A remark which would prove to be most prophetic.

The line of ascent was impaired by boulders and by a barricade built by the defenders. From within the caves that riddle the mountain the Zulus opened fire on the advancing force. Two officers and two men of the Frontier Light Horse fell.

Wood and his small party, on hearing the gunfire, hastened towards the plateau. Just below the summit they encountered Lieutenant-Colonel F.A. Weatherley and his Border Horse. Weatherley's men should have been with Buller but they had become separated, and had fallen in with Wood. As they climbed the heights, a Zulu shot dead Lloyd, the political assistant and the only Zulu speaker in the party. The shot which killed him tore into Wood's sleeve, and Wood's horse was also killed at this point. Wood ordered Weatherley to clear

105

the cave where the fire was coming from and Weatherley in turn ordered his men forward, but only Lieutenant J. Pool and Sub-Lieutenant H.W. Parminter responded to the command. Enraged by this, Captain the Hon R. Campbell, Coldstream Guards, Wood's staff officer, dashed forward, followed by Lieutenant H. Lysons, Private Fowler and three other mounted infantrymen of the 90th Light Infantry. As they reached the cave Campbell fell shot through the head. Lysons and his men stormed the cave in an attempt to flush out the Zulu snipers.

BREVET LIEUTENANT-
COLONEL R.H. BULLER,
60TH RIFLES

Under heavy fire Wood conducted a burial service for the two fallen men, fearful perhaps of the bodies being mutilated.

Weatherley's men continued their climb to the summit where Buller had been met by Lieutenant E.S. Browne, 1/24th Foot, and some twenty men of the mounted infantry. They had climbed the rugged path connecting the Ntendeka and Hlobane, on Russell's instructions, to inform Buller that Russell could not ascend the steep escarpment. Buller ordered Captain the Hon R.J. Barton, Coldstream Guards, commanding the

COMMANDANT P.L. UYS, WHOSE BURGHER FORCE WAS COMPOSED
OF HIS FAMILY AND FRIENDS, WILLINGLY RALLIED TO THE BRITISH CAUSE,
BUT HIS EXAMPLE WAS NOT FOLLOWED BY ANY OTHER BOER LEADER.

TROOPER H.B. GRANDIER, OF THE BORDER HORSE, TIED TO A STAKE. GRANDIER WAS THE ONLY MAN TO SURVIVE THE ORDEAL OF BEING TAKEN PRISONER OF WAR BY THE ZULU. SOME DOUBT HAS BEEN CAST ON GRANDIER'S TESTIMONY REGARDING HIS TREATMENT BY HIS CAPTORS: HE ALSO ALLEGED THAT HE ESCAPED HIS ESCORT AND RETURNED TO THE BRITISH LINES, BUT THIS IS A MATTER FOR CONJECTURE.

Frontier Light Horse, together with thirty men of the Frontier Light Horse, to bury the fallen of that corps, and also to locate Weatherley and his men. Scarcely had Barton set off, however, than Buller saw approaching from the south-east a Zulu army numbering about 20,000 men. Wood's attention had been drawn to the advancing impi by the frantic yells of his Zulu escort, who had no need of an interpreter to convey their words of warning.

Buller dispatched a note to Captain Barton 'to return by the right of the mountain', by which he had hoped to impress on Barton that he should make for Khambula. Sadly, the note when received by Barton, was misconstrued and he led his men, now joined by Weatherley's detachment, towards the Ityenka Nek, unwittingly straight into the Zulu impi. The small force were overwhelmed and Weatherley fell hand-in-hand with his fifteen-year-old son. Only a handful managed to evade the slaughter. Captain Barton took up Lieutenant Pool on his horse and rode off pursued by a number of Zulus, but after seven miles, Barton's horse floundered and both men were killed.

The Zulus on the summit, seeing that reinforcement was imminent, began harassing Buller's force. Buller ordered the levies down first and they scrambled down through the boulders and made off. About 100 levies died when they were overtaken by a wing of the impi. The descent was not so easy for the mounted men, as they slowly picked their way down leading their horses, and their escape down the appropriately nicknamed 'Devil's Pass' was hampered by fierce attacks by the Zulus.

Buller had expected support from Russell's force but owing to a misconstrued despatch from Wood, Russell had retired. The only assistance Buller's men received was from Browne and his mounted infantrymen. Buller rode back several times and rescued men who had lost their mounts from the very jaws of the Zulus. His example was followed by Browne, and by Major W.K. Leet of the 13th Light Infantry. Commandant P.L. Uys of the Burgher Force turned to offer assistance to one of his sons but was assegaied by Zulu who leapt on to his mount.

The British and Colonial forces withdrew in the direction of Khambula. Further resistance was futile, and the Zulus were left in possession of the field. It was about 12 noon.

Composition of the British Force

Brevet Colonel H.E. Wood, VC, 90th (Perthshire Volunteers) Light Infantry, commanding:

CAPTAIN THE
HON. R. CAMPBELL,
COLDSTREAM GUARDS

Staff: Captain the Hon R.G.E. Campbell, Coldstream Guards, Chief Staff Officer; Lieutenant H. Lysons, 90th Light Infantry, orderly officer; Mr L. Lloyd, political assistant and interpreter. Personal escort found by eight mounted infantrymen of the 90th Light Infantry and seven mounted 'friendly' Zulus. Captain H. Vaughan, Royal Artillery, Director of Transport

EASTERN PARTY
Brevet Lieutenant-Colonel R.H. Buller, CB, 60th Rifles commanding:
Staff Officer: Captain A.C. Gardner, 14th (King's) Hussars; Veterinary Surgeon F. Duck, 'N' Battery, 5th Brigade, Royal Artillery

11th Battery, 7th Brigade, Royal Artillery
A rocket party commanded by Major E.G. Tremlett, and seven other ranks

Burgher Force
Commanded by Commandant P.L. Uys and 32 volunteers

Frontier Light Horse
Commanded by Captain the Hon R.J. Barton, Coldstream Guards and Captain H.M.E. Brunker, 26th (Cameronians) Regiment of Foot and 156 officers and other ranks

LIEUTENANT-COLONEL
F.A. WEATHERLEY,
BORDER HORSE

Transvaal Rangers
Commanded by Commandant P.J. Raaf, 71 officers and other ranks

Border Horse
Commanded by Lieutenant-Colonel F.A. Weatherley, 53 officers and other ranks

Baker's Horse
Commanded by Lieutenant W.D. Wilson, 79 officers and other ranks

111

2nd Battalion of Wood's Irregulars
Commanded by Major W.K. Leet, 13th (Somerset) Light Infantry, 277 officers and other ranks

Lieutenant-Colonel (local rank) J.C. Russell, 12th (Prince of Wales' Royal) Lancers commanding:

11th Battery, 7th Brigade, Royal Artillery
A rocket party commanded by Lieutenant A.J. Bigge, and ten other ranks

1st Squadron Mounted Infantry
Commanded by Lieutenant E.S. Browne, 1st Battalion, 24th (2nd Warwickshires) Regiment of Foot and Lieutenant H.A. Walsh, 1st Battalion, 13th (Somerset) Light Infantry and 80 other ranks

Edendale Troop, Natal Native Horse
Commanded by Lieutenant W.F.D. Cochrane, 32nd (Cornwall) Light Infantry, 70 native other ranks

Kaffrarian Rifles
Commanded by Commandant F. Schermbrucker, 40 officers and other ranks

1st Battalion of Wood's Irregulars
Commanded by Commandant T.L. White, 240 officers and other ranks
200 followers of Prince Hamu kaNzibe, commanded by Lieutenant C.C. Williams, 58th (Rutlandshire) Regiment of Foot

British and Colonial Casualties

KILLED IN ACTION
Staff: Captain the Hon R.G.E. Campbell, Coldstream Guards; Mr L. Lloyd, Political Assistant and interpreter

Burgher Force
Commandant P.L. Uys

Frontier Light Horse
Captain the Hon R.J. Barton, Coldstream Guards (commanding the Frontier Light Horse)
Lieutenants: O. von Stietencron; G. Williams

(Compiler's Note: George Williams appears on the muster rolls of the Frontier Light Horse as Trooper (273) G. Williams. However, he held a commission as a captain in the 6th West Yorkshire Militia. He enlisted as a volunteer in the Frontier Light Horse on 1st January 1879. I can only conclude that his rank of lieutenant was attained due to his prior Militia service)

Corporals: G. Dodwell; H. Plante
Lance Corporal H. Runchman
Troopers: A.J. Burton; P.W. Caffin; A.W. Dobson; J. Gebser; W.

LIEUTENANT
G. WILLIAMS, FRONTIER
LIGHT HORSE

Gordon; J. Grills; T. Halliday; J. Hesseldine; E. Higgins; H. Hillwig; G. Horn; J. Kirwien; W.H. Livingstone; C. Lynden; J. May; M. Pendergast; D.A. Robson; W.A. Rogan; A. Schermel; G. Seymour; L. Shearer; A.L. Stewart; W. Tirrill.

Transvaal Rangers
Captain T.R. Hamilton
Troop Sergeant-Major W.H. Martin
Sergeant-Majors: T. Brophy; J.F. Cummings
Colour-Sergeant C. Stanley

Sergeant T. Berley
Trooper J. Beukes

Border Horse
Lieutenant-Colonel F.A. Weatherley
Adjutant V.H. Lys
Lieutenant J. Pool
Sub-Lieutenants: H.W. Parminter; R. Weatherley
Regimental Sergeant-Major E.J. Brown
Sergeant-Major J.S. Fisher

CAPTAIN
T.R. HAMILTON,
TRANSVAAL RANGERS

Quartermaster Sergeant F. Russell
Orderly Room Sergeant F.D. Brissenden
Paymaster Sergeant A. Johnson
Farrier-Major J. Freire
Trumpet-Major E.H. Meredith
Sergeant A. Stewart
Corporals: J. Blackmore; D. Coetzee; B. Ford; H.B. Porter; J.C. van
    Hasselt
Lance-Corporal E. Bernhardt
Trumpeter W. Reilly

LIEUTENANT J. POOL,
BORDER HORSE

ORDERLY ROOM
SERGEANT F.D.
BRISSENDEN, BORDER
HORSE

Troopers: L. Barth; C. Bourdoin; P.W. Brooks; J. Cameron; J.T. Craig; B.J. Craney; J. Darcy; W. Evans; H. Farquharson; A. Hartman; W. Jeffries; G. King; J.C. Mann; P. Martin; D. Milma; Jacob Muller; John Muller; F. Mulot; A. Reid; J. Shephard; Thompson; J. Underwood; F.G. Westhusan; Williams; S. Wynan

Baker's Horse
Troopers: J. Campbell; M. Christian; J. Darwin; R. Davis; W. Dunbar; J. Robinson; W. Walters; C. Ward

2nd Battalion of Wood's Irregulars
Lieutenant R. Dunscombe

Hamu kaNzibe's Followers
Lieutenant C.C. Williams, 58th (Rutlandshire) Regiment of Foot (commanding)
Mr Calverley

MISSING IN ACTION (presumed dead)
2nd Battalion of Wood's Irregulars
Captain C. Potter

MISSING IN ACTION (taken prisoner)
Border Horse
Trooper H.B. Grandier (also slightly wounded)

WOUNDED IN ACTION
1st Squadron Mounted Infantry
(Listed by parent unit)

2nd Battalion, 3rd (East Kent) Regiment of Foot ('The Buffs')
Private H. Weller, severely wounded

Frontier Light Horse
Troop Sergeant-Major J.A. D'Ewes, mortally wounded. Died of wounds 2nd April 1879
Corporal W. Brusseau, severely wounded
Trooper A. Rosser, slightly wounded
Trooper G. Mossop, slightly wounded

Transvaal Rangers
Trooper A. Tourkien, severely wounded
Trooper G. Vegeneiff, severely wounded

Border Horse
Trooper F. Hammond, severely wounded

Baker's Horse
Trooper W. Hutchins, severely wounded

Native Levies Casualties

KILLED IN ACTION
Approximately 100 natives from Wood's Irregulars and Hamu's people

Zulu Casualties

Details unknown

HONOURS AND AWARDS

The Victoria Cross
Captain and Brevet Lieutenant-Colonel Redvers H. BULLER, CB, 60th Rifles
The London Gazette
17th June 1879
For his gallant conduct at the retreat at Inhlobana [sic] on the 28th March 1879, in having assisted whilst hotly pursued by Zulus, in rescuing Captain C. D'Arcy, of the Frontier Light Horse, who was retiring on foot and carrying him on his horse until he overtook the rear guard. Also for having on the same date and under the same circumstances conveyed Lieutenant C. Everitt of the Frontier Light Horse, whose horse had been killed under him, to a place of safety. Later on, Colonel Buller, in the same manner, saved a trooper of the Frontier Light Horse whose horse was completely exhausted, and who otherwise would have been killed by the Zulus, who were within 80 yards of him.

*

Major William K. LEET, 1st Battalion, 13th Regiment
The London Gazette
17th June 1879
For his gallant conduct on the 28th March 1879, in rescuing from the

MAJOR W.K. LEET,
1ST/13TH LIGHT INFANTRY

PRIVATE E. FOWLER,
90TH LIGHT INFANTRY

Zulus Lieutenant A.M. Smith of the Frontier Light Horse, during the retreat from the Inhlobana [sic].

Lieutenant Smith, whilst on foot, his horse having been shot, was closely pursued by the Zulu, and would have been killed had not Major Leet taken him upon his horse and rode with him, under the fire of the enemy, to a place of safety.

*

Lieutenant Edward S. BROWNE, 1st Battalion, 24th Regiment
The London Gazette
17th June 1879
For his gallant conduct on the 29th March 1879 when the Mounted Infantry were being driven in by the enemy at Inhlobana [sic] in galloping back and twice assisting on his horse (under heavy fire and within a few yards of the enemy) one of the mounted men, who must otherwise have fallen into the enemy's hands.

*

Lieutenant H. LYSONS and Private E. FOWLER, 90th Light Infantry
   [At the time the *Gazette* was published the 90th had become the
   2nd Battalion of the Cameronians and Fowler had transferred to
   the Royal Irish Regiment.]
The London Gazette
5th April 1882
On the 28th March 1879, during the assault of the Inhlobane Mountain, [sic] Sir Evelyn Wood ordered the dislodgment of certain Zulus (who were causing the troops much loss) from strong natural caves commanding the position in which some of the wounded were laying. Some delay occurred in the execution of the orders issued. Captain the Hon Ronald Campbell, Coldstream Guards, followed by Lieutenant Lysons, Aide-de-Camp, and Private Fowler ran forward in the most determined manner, and advanced over a mass of fallen boulders and between walls of rock, which led to a cave in which the enemy lay hidden. It being impossible for two men to walk abreast, the assailants were consequently obliged to keep in single file, and as Captain Campbell was leading, he arrived first at the mouth of the cave, from which the Zulus were firing, and there met his death. Lieutenant Lysons and Private Fowler, who were following close behind him immediately dashed at the cave, from which led

TROOPER R. BROWN,
FRONTIER LIGHT HORSE

PRIVATE J. POWER,
1ST/24TH FOOT

several subterranean passages, and firing into the chasm below, succeeded in forcing the occupants to forsake their stronghold. Lieutenant Lysons remained at the cave's mouth for some minutes after the attack, during which time Captain Campbell's body was carried down the slopes.

The Silver Medal for Distinguished Conduct in the Field

Regiment/Corps	Name	Date of Submission
Frontier Light Horse	Corporal W.D. Vinnicombe	Sept 1879
Frontier Light Horse	Trooper R. Brown	Sept 1879
1st/24th Foot	Private J. Power	22/10/1879
90th Light Infantry	Bugler A. Walkinshaw	25/3/1882

VIII

The Zulu Assault on Wood's Encampment at Khambula
Saturday, 29th March 1879

'No quarter boys. Remember yesterday!'
– *Captain H.C.D. D'Arcy, Frontier Light Horse*

W OOD MADE preparations for a Zulu assault on Khambula, which became inevitable after the Hlobane fiasco. At
dawn on 29th March, a party of Raaf's Transvaal Rangers was
sent out on a reconnaissance. The party returned with one of
Hamu's followers, who had become detached in the confusion
at Hlobane. For his own safety he 'had turned his coat' and had
fallen in with his former companions from whom he gleaned
information regarding their intentions for Khambula.

Alerted by the intelligence, Wood prepared to receive an
imminent Zulu assault. At about 11 a.m. the Zulu columns
were sighted moving towards Khambula and at 12.45 p.m.,
after the men had eaten their lunch, Wood ordered the tents
struck and the men sent off to their positions. Boxes of reserve
ammunition were distributed. Everything possible had been
done to meet the onslaught. The only problem was that the
Zulu force appeared to have a different objective. Because of
the manoeuvering of the impi, Wood suspected that the threat
was directed towards Utrecht.

At about 1.30 p.m. Wood ordered out Buller and 100 of his
mounted troops to entice the Zulu into an attack on the
encampment. Buller dismounted his force within rifle range of
the oncoming Zulu and opened fire. Again, as at Isandlwana, it
was the inGobamakhosi who rushed forward. Buller's troops

remounted and fell back, only to halt again, dismount and engage the Zulu, before retiring on the encampment.

At about 1.45 p.m. the artillery pieces came crashing into action, but because of the nature of the terrain the cannon fire did not take its anticipated toll on the enemy. The Zulu right horn pressed on to within 300 yards, when they were checked by the rifle fire of Wood's own regiment, the 90th Light Infantry, and the Zulus were compelled to take cover.

Thirty minutes later, at 2.15 p.m., the Zulus launched a

BREVET COLONEL
H.E. WOOD, VC, 90TH
LIGHT INFANTRY

concerted attack as the centre and left horn advanced. The former assailed the south-east of the redoubt, whilst the latter moved in the dead ground below the south side of the laager. The uNdi 'corps' succeeded in driving out a company of the 1st/13th Light Infantry from the cattle kraal. From their newly occupied position the Zulus opened fire on the main laager. At this point about 1,000 warriors rushed forward intending to attack the main laager. Wood perceived the manoeuvre and ordered Brevet Major R.H. Hackett, commanding two companies of the 90th Light Infantry, to sally out and meet them at bayonet point. Hackett's determined advance broke the Zulu rush, who turned in retreat. Hackett's men then took up positions on the slope and poured volleys into the warriors. To add to the Zulu casualties the Royal Artillery cannon opened fire on them. The guns also swept the cattle laager, causing the Zulus to abandon their position there.

Hackett fell severely wounded, blinded by a round which entered one temple and exited through the other and a fierce cross-fire caused his men to retreat into the safety of the main laager. Almost simultaneously with Hackett's foray, a company of the 13th Light Infantry had moved out of the south-west corner of the main laager to meet a Zulu rush at bayonet point but the sortie was driven back by the warriors of umCiyo's regiment.

For two hours, with extreme courage, the Zulus relentlessly assaulted the encampment. At about 4.30 p.m. attacks were made on the north and north-eastern faces of the camp, only to be held back by the defenders. By 5 p.m. the intensity of the Zulu assaults was faltering and at 5.30 p.m. Wood ordered a company of the 13th Light Infantry, supported by a company of the 90th Light Infantry to clear the cattle laager. The Zulu attackers were driven off at bayonet point, whilst the cannon pounded the Zulu with cannister. The Zulus now fell back and retreated in disarray.

Wood ordered Brevet Lieutenant-Colonel R.H. Buller to pursue the retreating Zulu with his mounted men. Captain H.C.D. D'Arcy, of the Frontier Light Horse, bellowed out, 'No quarter boys – remember yesterday.' The pursuit was relentless and hundreds of Zulus were ridden down and killed. Hlobane had certainly been avenged. The last of the mounted troops returned to Khambula at about 9 p.m.

Composition of the British Force

Brevet Colonel H.E. Wood, 90th (Perthshire Volunteers) Light Infantry, commanding:

Staff: Captain E.R.P. Woodgate, 4th (The King's Own) Regiment of Foot; Captain A.B. Maude, 90th; Captain H. Vaughan, Royal Artillery, Director of Transport; Lieutenant F. Smith, 90th Light Infantry; Lieutenant H. Lysons, 90th Light Infantry; Surgeons J. O'Reilly and A.L. Brown, Army Medical Department; Veterinary-Surgeon F. Duck, 'N' Battery, 5th Brigade, Royal Artillery; Deputy Commissary E. Hughes; Assistant Commissaries R.A. Chermside, W.J.B. Bampfield, F.St.J. Fagan and J. Whitley, Commissariat and Transport Department

LIEUTENANT
F. NICOLSON, RA

11th Battery, 7th Brigade, Royal Artillery
Major E.G. Tremlett commanding:
Captain A.J. Bigge
Lieutenants: F.G. Slade; F. Nicolson
and 106 other ranks (includes attached other ranks)

Royal Engineers
11 other ranks

1st Battalion 13th (Somerset) Light Infantry
Lieutenant-Colonel P.E.V. Gilbert commanding:

Major E.L. England

Captains: J.F. James; W. Cox; D.T. Perssé; G.H.A. Kinloch; W.H. Evans; H.H. Thurlow; J.M.E. Waddy; E.J. Gallway (Adjutant)

Lieutenants: E.W. Clark; R.A.H. Townsend; E.M. Poynton; A.G. Wilbraham; R. Levinge; R.B. Williams; A.W.A. Pollock; R.L. Payne; G.A. Pardoe

2nd Lieutenants: J.W.H. West; H.W. Lovett

and 507 other ranks

90th (Perthshire Volunteers) Light Infantry
Brevet Lieutenant-Colonel R.M. Rogers, vc commanding:

Majors: A. Cherry; R.H. Hackett; R.I. Ward

Captains: W.S. Hamilton; W.F. Wilson; R. Lawrence; G.W. Hutchinson; G.R. Heathcote

Lieutenants: S.H. Lomax (Adjutant); F. Smith; P.E.C. Sheehan; A. Gordon; S.P. Strong; H.E. Hothan; A.O. White; J. Ross; C.H.I. Hopkins; R.B. Fell

2nd Lieutenant A.T. Bright

Paymaster F. Taylor

Quartermaster J. Newman

and 690 other ranks

Wood's Irregulars
58 all ranks commanded by Major W.K. Leet, 13th (Somerset) Light Infantry

Brevet Lieutenant-Colonel R.H. Buller, 60th Rifles, commanding a mounted force comprising:

1st Squadron Mounted Infantry
Commanded by Lieutenant-Colonel J.C. Russell, 12th (Prince of Wales' Royal) Lancers

Captains: A.C. Gardner, 14th (Kings) Hussars; R.H. McCarthy, 2nd Battalion, 4th (King's Own) Regiment

Lieutenants: N. Newnham-Davis, 2nd Battalion, 3rd (East Kent) Regiment of Foot ('The Buffs'); H.A. Walsh, 1st Battalion, 13th (Somerset) Light Infantry; E.S. Browne, 1st Battalion, 24th (2nd Warwickshire) Regiment of Foot

and 93 other ranks

Frontier Light Horse
Commanded by Captain H.C.D. D'Arcy

Captains: H.M.E. Brunker, 26th (Cameronians) Regiment of Foot; J.E.H. Prior, 80th Regiment of Foot
and 106 officers and other ranks

Transvaal Rangers
Commanded by Commandant P.J. Raaf, 134 officers and other ranks

Baker's Horse
Commanded by Commandant F.J. Baker, 90 officers and other ranks

Kaffrarian Rifles
Commanded by Commandant F. Schermbrucker, 39 officers and other ranks

Burgher Force
Ten men

Border Horse
16 all ranks

Edendale Troop, Natal Native Horse
Commanded by Lieutenant W.F.D. Cochrane, 32nd (Cornwall) Light Infantry, 73 officers and other ranks, natives and Europeans

British and Colonial Casualties

KILLED IN ACTION
1st Battalion, 13th (Somerset) Light Infantry
Privates: W. Arthur; J. Collins; J. Duncan; J. Hayes; S. Montgomery

90th (Perthshire Volunteers) Light Infantry
Colour-Sergeant T.H. McAllen (This non-commissioned officer was initially wounded in action but having had his wound dressed he returned to the fight and was killed.)
Privates: J. Fairclough; J. McLean; R. Murphy; W. Peace; J. Richardson; W. Spence

1st Squadron Mounted Infantry
(Listed by parent unit)

2nd Battalion, 3rd (East Kent) Regiment of Foot ('The Buffs')
Private C. Moore

Frontier Light Horse
Sergeant J. Tibbits
Trooper C. Merk

Contractor's Agent
Mr J. Ferreira

MORTALLY WOUNDED
11th Battery, 7th Brigade, Royal Artillery
Lieutenant F. Nicolson, died of wounds 30th March 1879
Gunner H. McCann, died of wounds 11th April 1879

1st Battalion, 13th (Somerset) Light Infantry
Privates: E. Blakeman, died of wounds 23rd May 1879; W. Grovs-
    nor, died of wounds; W. Kearney, died of wounds 1st April 1879;
    W. McNulty, died of wounds 2nd April 1879; P. Mooney, died of
    wounds 5th April 1879; S. Redpath, died of wounds 29th March
    1879

90th (Perthshire Volunteers) Light Infantry
2nd Lieutenant A.T. Bright, died of wounds 29th March 1879
Privates: J. Bryan; J. Chapman; H. Gilbert; P. Ryan

Transvaal Rangers
Lieutenant J. White, died of wounds 1st April 1879

Burgher Force
Trooper L.S. Combrink, died of wounds 26th April 1879

Native Mule Driver
Unknown

WOUNDED IN ACTION
1st Battalion, 13th (Somerset) Light Infantry
Captains: W. Cox, severely wounded; D.T. Perssé, severely wound-
    ed
Colour Sergeant A. Fricker, severely wounded
Sergeant J. Woods, severely wounded
Bugler J. Clery, slightly wounded
Privates: W. Bellancy, slightly wounded; J. Cogan, slightly wound-
    ed; G. Davies, severely wounded; D. Foster, dangerously wound-
    ed; J. Harkness, slightly wounded; A. Hayball; dangerously
    wounded; J. Madden, severely wounded; G. Medlem, severely

wounded; G. Nutt, dangerously wounded; H. Roberts, slightly wounded; J. Stevens, slightly wounded; W.J. Todd, severely wounded

80th (Staffordshire Volunteers) Regiment of Foot attached to 11th Battery, 7th Brigade, Royal Artillery
Sergeant T. Brown, severely wounded

90th (The Perthshire Volunteers) Light Infantry
Brevet Major R.H. Hackett, dangerously wounded
Lieutenant S.J. Smith, severely wounded

2ND LIEUTENANT
A.T. BRIGHT, 90TH
LIGHT INFANTRY

Corporals: C. Delaney, severely wounded; R.L. Grey, slightly wounded
Privates: J.R. Branch, severely wounded; H. Butler, severely wounded; J. Connors, dangerously wounded; J. Daly, dangerously wounded; H. Ferguson, severely wounded; J. Forbes, slightly wounded; W. Jones, severely wounded; J. Mead, severely wounded; T. Mealey, severely wounded; J. Miller, slightly wounded; D. Morgan, slightly wounded; J. Morris, slightly wounded; M. Mullins, severely wounded; G. Peacock, dangerously wounded; W. Reason, dangerously wounded; P. Rispin, slightly wounded; J.

Shea, slightly wounded; C. Shears, slightly wounded; J. Smith, slightly wounded

1st Squadron Mounted Infantry
(Listed by parent units)

14th (King's) Hussars
Captain A.C. Gardener, severely wounded

4th (The King's Own) Regiment of Foot
Private J. Anderson, slightly wounded
Private R. Bestwick, severely wounded

80th (Staffordshire Volunteers) Regiment of Foot
Corporal W. Thompson, severely wounded

Frontier Light Horse
Trooper T.H. Peterson, dangerously wounded
Trooper T.A.B. Stopforth, severely wounded
Trooper Sulmontein, severely wounded

Baker's Horse
Trooper R. Crichton, slightly wounded

Kaffrarian Rifles
Trooper J. Hansen, dangerously wounded

Edendale Troop, Natal Native Horse
Trooper Seeke, severely wounded

Native Mule Drivers
Two unknown natives severely wounded

Zulu Casualties

Approximately 1,500 killed/mortally wounded

HONOURS AND AWARDS

The Silver Medal for Distinguished Conduct in the Field

Regiment/Corps	Name	Date of Submission
11th/7th Royal Artillery	Acting Sergeant E. Quigley	13/8/1881

1st/13th (The Somerset) Light Infantry	Private A. Page	27/5/1879
Natal Native Horse (Edendale Troop)	Troop Sergeant-Major Learda	18/9/1879

IX

The Siege of Eshowe
Thursday, 23rd January 1879
–Thursday, 3rd April 1879

'Cut off from the land that bore us'
– *Contemporary song: 'Here's to the Next Man Who Dies'*

FOLLOWING HIS victory at Nyezane, Colonel C.K. Pearson made for the abandoned mission station at Eshowe. From the day of his arrival, he took steps to prepare the mission station for defence, a task the local Zulus impeded by firing on the work parties.

On 28th January, Pearson received news of the Isandlwana massacre together with orders from Chelmsford to act as he saw fit: to remain or return to the Tugela. After a conference with his officers he decided to stay. He did, however, instruct his mounted troops and native contingent to retire to the Tugela, for want of adequate provisions for them. That same evening Colonel H.F.W. Ely of the 99th Regiment of Foot arrived with a convoy of provisions and ammunition.

Two days later, Pearson endeavoured to send out three messengers to communicate with the forces stationed on the Tugela. However they were compelled to return to Eshowe because of the numbers of Zulu barring the route. On the same day a party of natives, whom Pearson had ordered to escort a large number of oxen, were surprised and their stock captured.

The next day, the 31st, Zulus were sighted on a hill overlooking the mission station. They were promptly shelled by artillery and driven from their position. However, the cramped conditions of the 'Fort' began to take its toll on the health of

132

THE FORTIFIED MISSION STATION AT ESHOWE

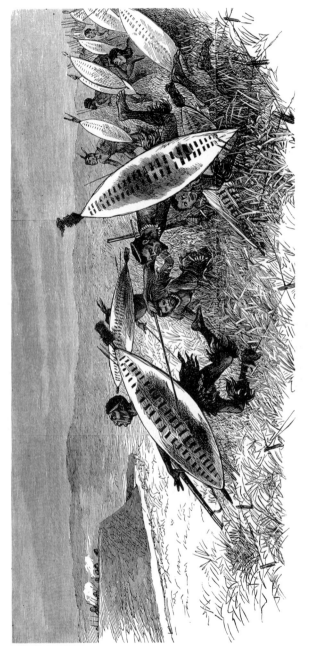

A ZULU ATTACK IS REPULSED BY SUSTAINED FIRING FROM THE REVETMENT AT ESHOWE

BY USE OF A CONTRIVED SYSTEM OF MIRRORS REFLECTING THE SUN'S
RAYS, THE DEFENDERS OF ESHOWE WERE ABLE TO MAINTAIN HELIOGRAPHIC
COMMUNICATION WITH THEIR RELIEF FORCE

the men and on 1st February a private of the 3rd Regiment of Foot died from fever. The picquets and outposts came under fire from besieging Zulus. With the British forced to remain inside the confines of the mission, the sanitary arrangements led to an outbreak of dysentery. As February wore on, it was disease not enemy action that extracted its mortal toll, and the medical supplies dwindled. Intensive storms raged, adding to the general despair.

On 21st February a force of some 200 men, supported by a rocket party, moved out to dislodge the Zulus who were pestering the cattle guard – but to no avail. The claustrophobic effects of the siege proved too much for Private W. Knee, 99th Regiment of Foot, who took his own life by drowning.

At 2 a.m. on 1st March a party of 500 men, supported by one artillery piece, marched out and successfully destroyed a military kraal, some seven miles from Eshowe. The party returned at 10.30 a.m., having accomplished their mission without sustaining casualties. On the following day, 2nd March, the garrison was encouraged by sighting heliograph signals from the direction of the mission station of St Andrews. Further messages were transmitted over the next few days which intimated that relief was almost at hand.

A vedette was surprised on 7th March by eleven Zulus and Corporal S. Carson, 99th Regiment of Foot was severely wounded. A party working on cutting a new road was constantly harassed by the Zulus. Fortunately they only received one casualty: on 11th March Lieutenant D.F. Lewis, 3rd Regiment of Foot, was slightly wounded by a bullet which passed through his helmet and grazed his forehead. Private W. Kent, 99th Regiment of Foot, was not so lucky. During the night of 16th/17th March he was killed whilst on sentry-go. When his body was recovered it was found to be riddled with eighteen assegai wounds.

Further heliograph signals informed the garrison that a relief force would leave the Tugela on 1st April. The garrison, however, had already observed large Zulu troop movements. Eshowe would not be relieved without a fight!

Casualties of the Siege of Eshowe

(in date order)

1st February 1879
2nd Battalion, 3rd (East Kent) Regiment of Foot ('The Buffs')
Private A. Kingston, died of fever

11th February 1879
HMS Active
Shoemaker J. Moore, died from dysentery

COLONEL C.K. PEARSON,
3RD FOOT

13th February 1879
2nd Battalion, 3rd (East Kent) Regiment of Foot ('The Buffs')
Private W. McLeod, died from dysentery

15th February 1879
2nd Battalion, 3rd (East Kent) Regiment of Foot ('The Buffs')
Private E. Oakley, died from diarrhoea

21st February 1879
2nd Battalion, 3rd (East Kent) Regiment of Foot ('The Buffs')
Lance-Corporal T. Taylor, died from dysentery

99th The Duke of Edinburgh's (Lanarkshire) Regiment of Foot
Private J. Shields, died from dysentery
Private W. Knee, suicide by drowning

4th March 1879
99th The Duke of Edinburgh's (Lanarkshire) Regiment of Foot
Private J. Paul, died from the effects of sunstroke

6th March 1879
2nd Battalion, 3rd (East Kent) Regiment of Foot ('The Buffs')
Drummer A. Mortimer, died from dysentery

8th March 1879
HMS Active
Leading Seaman J. Radford, died of fever

Army Hospital Corps
Private W. Barber, died of fever

9th March 1879
2nd Battalion, 3rd (East Kent) Regiment of Foot ('The Buffs')
Private J. Stack, died of an intestinal obstruction

12th March 1879
2nd Battalion, 3rd (East Kent) Regiment of Foot ('The Buffs')
Captain H.J.N. Williams, died of fever

16th March 1879
99th The Duke of Edinburgh's (Lanarkshire) Regiment of Foot
Private W. Tubb, died from the effects of sunstroke

HMS Active
Midshipman L.C. Coker, died from typhoid
Marine W. Stagg, died from pneumonia

16th/17th March 1879
99th The Duke of Edinburgh's (Lanarkshire) Regiment of Foot
Private W. Kent, killed in action on sentry duty

17th March 1879
99th The Duke of Edinburgh's (Lanarkshire) Regiment of Foot
Private T. Venn, died from enteric fever

21st March 1879
99th The Duke of Edinburgh's (Lanarkshire) Regiment of Foot
Private C. Coombes, died from enteric fever

26th March 1879
99th The Duke of Edinburgh's (Lanarkshire) Regiment of Foot
Private P. Roden, died from enteric fever

27th March 1879
2nd Battalion, 3rd (East Kent) Regiment of Foot ('The Buffs')
Private A. Tarrant, died from bronchitis

99th The Duke of Edinburgh's (Lanarkshire) Regiment of Foot
Lieutenant A.S.F. Davidson, died from enteric fever

LIEUTENANT
G.R.J. EVELYN,
2ND/3RD FOOT

28th March 1879
99th The Duke of Edinburgh's (Lanarkshire) Regiment of Foot
Private B. Lewis, died from enteric fever

31st March 1879
2nd Battalion, 3rd (East Kent) Regiment of Foot ('The Buffs')
Lieutenant G.R.J. Evelyn, died from enteric fever

2nd April 1879
HMS Active
Able-Seaman A. Smith, died of fever

4th April 1879
2nd Battalion, 3rd (East Kent) Regiment of Foot ('The Buffs')
Private J. Monk, died from enteric fever

7th March 1879
99th The Duke of Edinburgh's (Lanarkshire) Regiment of Foot
Corporal S. Carson, severely wounded

11th March 1879
2nd Battalion, 3rd (East Kent) Regiment of Foot ('The Buffs')
Lieutenant D.F. Lewis, slightly wounded

X

The Battle of Gingindlovu
Wednesday, 2nd April 1879

'They all thought to catch us napping, but they
found us awake' – *Captain C.J. Matthews,
57th (West Middlesex) Regiment of Foot*

FOLLOWING CHELMSFORD's plea for reinforcements after
the Isandlwana reverse, by March the first of these had
begun to arrive. Chelmsford now prepared to take the field,
making use of these fresh troops. His main anxiety was to
extricate Pearson's besieged column at Eshowe and for this
purpose the Eshowe Relief Column was formed, in two brigades. It crossed the Tugela River on 28th March, coinciding
with the date Chelmsford had ordered Wood to create a
diversion in his theatre of operations – the assault on Hlobane.
Hampered by appalling weather the force advanced into
Zululand.

Caution dictated Chelmsford's strategy: mindful of surprise
attacks he ordered each halting place to be laagered and
entrenched. Mounted troops rode in advance of the force for
the purpose of reconnoitring the disposition of the Zulu. On
Tuesday, 1st April, the column laagered and entrenched near
to the destroyed military kraal of Gingindlovu. During the
evening the mounted patrols reported that Zulu forces were
congregating in the vicinity of Umisi Hill. To confirm this John
Dunn, 'The White Zulu', undertook a daring lone reconnaissance towards the Zulu position. On his return he reported
seeing the Zulu's bivouac fires but was unable to assess their
precise strength.

The troops within the laager spent a restless night. The

RATINGS OF THE NAVAL BRIGADES, WHICH FOUGHT AT GINGINDLOVU

MEN OF THE 2ND SQUADRON MOUNTED INFANTRY RELENTLESSLY HARRY THE FLEEING ZULU

AS THE RELIEF COLUMN MARCHES INTO ESHOWE, IT IS CHEERED ON
BY A GROUP OF INVALIDS, PICTURED LEFT, OBVIOUSLY THANKFUL THAT THEY DID NOT SUFFER
THE FATE OF THEIR COMRADES WHOSE GRAVES ARE DEPICTED

majority were untried young men and fear of the unknown caused at least one false alarm. At 5 a.m. on Wednesday, 2nd April, a heavy mist cloaked the laager. Chelmsford ordered out his mounted men to scout the area for the whereabouts of the Zulu and a patrol of Natal Native Horse, under the command of Captain C. Nourse, the Isandlwana survivor, sighted the enemy crossing the Nyezane River and advancing on the laager. A smattering of shots were fired and the mounted troops withdrew into the laager. At 6 a.m. stand-to was

JOHN DUNN, 'THE WHITE ZULU' A FORMER FAVOURITE OF KING CETSHWAYO

ordered and the troops were told, 'No independent firing – volleys by companies when they are within three hundred yards'. These were virtually the only orders issued.

The Zulus deployed into their usual horned formation, the left horn advancing in two columns. The Gatling gun commander, positioned at the north-east corner of the laager, implored permission to open-up on a body of Zulus forming up to his front. His request was overheard by Chelmsford who permitted a short burst to test the range, which the gun commander knew to be 800 yards. The Gatling roared into action and with a cyclic rate of fire of 200 rounds per minute cut a swath through the Zulus with just two cranks of the handle.

The Zulus pressed their attack by attempting to envelop the laager. Mindful of their orders, the troops opened fire at the designated range. Crashing volleys vied with the chatter of the Gatlings, cannon fire with the whoosh of rockets.

Undaunted the Zulus still pressed their attacks. The inexperienced Riflemen of the 3rd Battalion of the 60th Rifles (The King's Royal Rifle Corps) were apparently unnerved. To add to their dismay, their commanding officer, Brevet Lieutenant-Colonel F.V. Northey, was struck in the shoulder by a bullet. He withdrew to have the round removed and then returned to his command but while encouraging his men he haemorrhaged and fell with blood spraying from his brachial artery. Despite the ferocity of the assaults the Zulus failed to get within 25 yards of the laager, save for one uDibi boy (a supply carrier), aged no more than twelve years, who eluded the fire only to be taken captive by a rating of HMS *Boadicea*.

At about 6.45 a.m., having sustained heavy casualties, the Zulus began to fall back. Seizing his opportunity, Chelmsford ordered Brevet Major P.H.S. Barrow to lead out his mounted troops in pursuit, which he did relentlessly. Commandant W.J. Nettleton's 5th Battalion of the Natal Native Contingent joined in the rout and set about butchering the Zulu wounded. Adding to the devastation, the artillery shelled the retreating Zulus.

The action was concluded by 7.30 a.m. Eshowe was relieved on Thursday, 3rd April 1879 and Pearson's ordeal was over.

The Composition of the British Force

Lieutenant-General Lord Chelmsford commanding:

Staff: Brevet Lieutenant-Colonel J.N. Crealock, 95th (Derbyshire) Regiment of Foot, Military Secretary; Captain W.C.F. Molyneux, 22nd (Cheshire) Regiment of Foot and Lieutenant A.B. Milne,

HMS *Active*, aides-de-camp; Brigade Surgeon T. Tarrant, Army Medical Department, Senior Medical Officer; Deputy Commissary C.E. Walton, Commissariat and Transport Department, Senior Commissariat Officer; The Honourable W. Drummond and Mr J. Dunn, Intelligence Department

1st Brigade
Lieutenant-Colonel F.T.A. Law, Royal Artillery, commanding:
Staff Officer: Captain A.F. Hart, 31st (Huntingdonshire) Regiment of Foot

BREVET LIEUTENANT-COLONEL J.N. CREALOCK, 95TH FOOT

2nd Battalion, 3rd (East Kent) Regiment of Foot ('The Buffs')
Detachment commanded by Major A.L. Walker, 99th Duke of Edinburgh's (Lanarkshire) Regiment of Foot
Captains: W.H. Wyldd; H.W. Maclear; J.B. Backhouse
Lieutenant A.J.W. Allen
Second-Lieutenant A.H. Tylden-Pattenson
and 135 other ranks

91st (Princess Louise's Argyllshire) Highlanders
Lieutenant-Colonel A.C. Bruce, commanding:
Brevet Lieutenant-Colonel W.P. Gurney

147

Captains: G.N. Stevenson; G.L. O'Sullivan; J. Boulderson; W.R.H. Craufurd; D.J. MacG. MacDonald; J.T. Rogers; W. Prevost; W.S. Mills; H.G. Fallowfield

Lieutenants: J.L.C. St. Clair; A.E.H. Tottenham; G.D. Collings; H.F.C. Johnston; G.B. Robbins; D.G.M. Fowler; G.L.J. Goff

Second-Lieutenants: T. Fraser; C.J. Richardson

Quartermaster J. Gillies

and 829 other ranks

99th The Duke of Edinburgh's (Lanarkshire) Regiment of Foot
Major A.L. Walker commanding:

Captains: A.M'A. Moir; F.L. Story; C.H.S. Kennedy; J.M. Hanson

Lieutenants: A.W. Turner; C.H. Alexander

Second-Lieutenants: J.S. Guille; C.F.G. Young; C.LeG. Justice; F.P. Cockburn; A. Elderton; W.I. D'Arcy

Attached: Second-Lieutenant M.W. Gavin, 21st Hussars

and 417 other ranks

Naval Landing Brigade from HMS Shah
Commander J. Brackenbury commanding:

Commander M.H. Drummond commanding the Gatling gun and Artillery Detachment

Lieutenant (Gunnery) C. Lindsay

Lieutenants: G.P. Henderson; T.P. Abbott, The Hon P.M. Hely-Hutchinson

Sub-Lieutenants: F.S. Hamilton; A.H. Smith-Dorrien

Staff Surgeon J. Shields

Surgeons: T.M. Sibbald and J.J. Connell

Clerk J.H.G. Chapple

Gunners (Petty Officer Rate): D. O'Neil, J. Cook

Boatswain T. Hammet

and 335 ratings

4th Battalion Natal Native Contingent
Commanded by Captain G. Barton, 7th (Royal Fusiliers) Regiment of Foot

800 all ranks, natives and Europeans

2nd Brigade
Lieutenant-Colonel W.L. Pemberton, 3rd Battalion, 60th Rifles (King's Royal Rifle Corps) commanding:

Staff Officer: Captain E.H. Buller, The Rifle Brigade

57th (West Middlesex) Regiment of Foot
Lieutenant-Colonel C.M. Clarke, commanding:
Major H.D. Bicknell
Captains: C.J. Matthews; H.C. Hinxman; A.A.D. Weigall; G. Dewar
Lieutenants: A.A. Garstin; A.W. Hill; J.G. White; R.W. Graham; S.E. Bellingham; E.V. Bellers; R.D. Longe; E.J. Sharpe; W. Scott-Moncrieff; C.W. Warden; A. Towers-Clark
Second-Lieutenants: H. James; L.W. Bodé
Quartermaster T. Wood
and 620 other ranks

3rd Battalion, 60th Rifles (King's Royal Rifle Corps)
Brevet Lieutenant-Colonel F.V. Northey commanding:
Captains: C.P. Cramer; A.V. O'Brien; E.T.H. Hutton; A.H. Bircham; K. Turnour; C. Mitchell
Lieutenants: G. Astell; E.O.H. Wilkinson; R.H. Gunning; A.P. Crawley
Second-Lieutenants: G.C.B. Baker; A.C. Baskerville Mynors
Quartermaster J. Ireland
Attached: Lieutenant H. Allfrey, 1st Battalion, 60th Rifles
and 525 other ranks

Naval Landing Brigade from HMS Boadicea
Commodore T.W. Richards commanding:
Staff: Lieutenant H. Preedy (aide-de-camp)
Commander A. Kingscote commanding the Artillery Detachment
Senior Lieutenant (Gunnery) F.R. Carr, commanding the Rocket Battery
Staff-Surgeon W.D. Longfield
Lieutenants: E.C. Hobkirk; J.B. Benett; H. Lyon
Sub-Lieutenant J. Startin
Acting Sub-Lieutenant G.J.S. Warrender
Midshipmen: W.W. Hewett; A.F. Crookshank; The Hon S.C. Colville
and 178 ratings

Royal Marines
Royal Marine Artillery:
Captain A.L.S. Burrowes
Royal Marine Light Infantry:

149

Captain J. Phillips
Lieutenant J.W. Robyns
and 97 RMA and RMLI other ranks drawn from *Boadicea* and *Shah*

5th Battalion Natal Native Contingent
Commanded by Commandant W.F. Nettleton
1,200 all ranks, natives and Europeans

Divisional Troops
Brevet Major P.H.S. Barrow, 19th Hussars commanding:
Staff Officer: Lieutenant E.R. Courtenay, 20th Hussars

2nd Squadron Mounted Infantry
Captain W. Sugden, 1st Battalion, 24th (2nd Warwickshires) Regiment of Foot
Captain (local rank) H. de C. Rawlins, 90th (Perthshire Volunteers) Light Infantry
Lieutenant F. Cookson, 91st (Argyllshire) Highlanders
and 67 other ranks drawn from regular units

No. 2 Troop Natal Horse
Commanded by Captain J.W. Cooke
and 30 all ranks

Natal Volunteer Guides
Commanded by Captain F. Addison, Stanger Mounted Rifles
and 50 all ranks drawn from various Natal volunteer corps

Natal Native Horse
Jantzi's Horse and Mafunzi's Horse:
130 native all ranks

John Dunn's Native Foot Scouts
150 natives

British and Colonial Casualties

KILLED IN ACTION
3rd Battalion, 60th Rifles (King's Royal Rifle Corps)
Private J. Pratt

91st (Princess Louise's Argyllshire) Highlanders
Private R. Marshall

99th The Duke of Edinburgh's (Lanarkshire) Regiment of Foot
Privates: J. Lawrence; J. Smith

Natal Native Contingent
Four native other ranks

Natal Native Horse (Jantzi's Horse)
One native trooper

MORTALLY WOUNDED
57th (West Middlesex) Regiment of Foot
Private T. Perkins, died of wounds 19th April 1879

BREVET LIEUTENANT-
COLONEL F.V. NORTHEY,
60TH RIFLES

3rd Battalion, 60th Rifles (King's Royal Rifle Corps)
Brevet Lieutenant-Colonel F.V. Northey, died of wounds 6th April
    1879

99th The Duke of Edinburgh's (Lanarkshire) Regiment of Foot
Lieutenant G.C.J. Johnson, died of wounds 2nd April 1879
Private P. Armstrong
Private G. Baker

Natal Native Contingent
Two native other ranks

WOUNDED IN ACTION
Staff
95th (Derbyshire) Regiment of Foot
Brevet Lieutenant-Colonel J.N. Crealock, slightly wounded

57th (West Middlesex) Regiment of Foot
Captain H.C. Hinxman, slightly wounded
Private J. Deacon, slightly wounded
Private J. Harris, slightly wounded

3rd Battalion, 60th Rifles (King's Royal Rifle Corps)
Colour Sergeant E. Dallard, slightly wounded

LIEUTENANT
G.C.J. JOHNSON,
99TH FOOT

Privates: F. Aylett, slightly wounded; E. France, slightly wounded; J. Franey, slightly wounded; M. Lassiff, dangerously wounded; W. Poplett, dangerously wounded

91st (Princess Louise's Argyllshire) Highlanders
Sergeant J. McIntyre, dangerously wounded
Drummer H. Stanridge, slightly wounded
Privates: J. Bryan, dangerously wounded; P. Gillespie, severely wounded; P. Hanlon, dangerously wounded; C. McIntyre, dangerously wounded; J. Malley, dangerously wounded; M. Richards, severely wounded; R. Sutton, severely wounded

99th The Duke of Edinburgh's (Lanarkshire) Regiment of Foot
Privates: J. Blackwell, slightly wounded; J. Drew, dangerously wounded

2nd Squadron Mounted Infantry
(Listed by parent units)

19th Hussars
Brevet Major P.H.S. Barrow, slightly wounded

88th (Connaught Rangers) Regiment of Foot
Private D. Bryan, slightly wounded

90th (Perthshire Volunteers) Light Infantry
Private A. Hartley, severely wounded

Naval Landing Brigade from HMS Shah
Petty Officer J. Porteous (seconded from HMS *Tenedos*), slightly wounded
Able Seamen: E. Bird, severely wounded; J. Bulger, severely wounded

Naval Landing Brigade from HMS Boadicea
Staff Surgeon W.D. Longfield, dangerously wounded
Bugler Boy J. Hinchley, dangerously wounded
Carpenter's Mate P. Condy, slightly wounded

Royal Marine Artillery
Acting-Bombardier G. Parfitt, dangerously wounded

4th Battalion Natal Native Contingent
Six unnamed native other ranks, details of wounds unknown

5th Battalion Natal Native Contingent
Eight unnamed native other ranks, severely wounded

Natal Native Horse (Mafunzi's Horse)
One native trooper, severely wounded

Zulu Casualties

Approximately 1,200 killed. One prisoner taken alive

XI

The Ambush of the Prince Imperial
Ityotyozi River
Sunday, 1st June 1879

'How many hundred unknown mothers mourn
slain sons? Why should this one our hearts so stir?'
— *Punch*

IN THE wake of the Isandlwana disaster, a certain young man implored permission from His Royal Highness the Duke of Cambridge, Commander-in-Chief of the British Army, to accompany the reinforcements. That young man was His Imperial Highness Eugène Louis Jean Joseph Napoleon Bonaparte, the exiled Prince Imperial of France and son of Napoleon III.

Louis, as he was commonly known, had lived a life of exile in England following the defeat of his father's armies in the Franco-Prussian War. At the age of sixteen he entered the Royal Military Academy, Woolwich, where officer-cadets of the Corps of Royal Engineers and the Royal Regiment of Artillery were instructed. Louis graduated from the Academy in the autumn of 1875 but, because of his position, he was not commissioned into the British Army, merely allowed to perform duties as an honorary lieutenant in the Royal Artillery.

With the coming of the Zulu War many of the Prince's peers from Woolwich were assigned to active service. Louis longed to share the rigours of active service that his friends were enduring. He sought permission to serve with the Royal Artillery, but his offer was declined. His persistence was rewarded when he was allowed to join Chelmsford's staff as an

154

THE PRINCE IMPERIAL OF FRANCE, HIS IMPERIAL HIGHNESS
EUGENE LOUIS JEAN JOSEPH NAPOLEON BONAPARTE ON A RECONNAISSANCE
IN ZULULAND. THE PRINCE IS DEPICTED WEARING THE UNDRESS
UNIFORM OF AN OFFICER IN THE ROYAL ARTILLERY.

THE PRINCE IMPERIAL AND HIS PARTY LANGUISH IN THE DESERTED
KRAAL, BLISSFULLY UNAWARE OF THE IMPENDING DANGER.

AS THE PRINCE'S COFFIN, BORNE ON A GUN-CARRIAGE, PASSES, THE ASSEMBLED
TROOPS HAVE BEEN CALLED TO THE 'REVERSE-ARMS' POSITION AS A SIGN OF MOURNING.

extra aide-de-camp. He left England on 27th February 1879 on board *The Danube*, eventually reaching Natal on 9th April.

Owing to a bout of fever, Louis did not take up his position until 2nd May; inhibited by the lack of action that his duties permitted, he sought permission to be engaged on more arduous tasks. He was consequently assigned to the staff of Brevet Colonel R. Harrison, Royal Engineers, who had recently been appointed as Assistant Quartermaster-General. Louis busied himself about his new duties, under the supervision of the Deputy Assistant Quartermaster-General, Lieutenant J.B. Carey of the 98th (The Prince of Wales') Regiment of Foot. Louis' skills as a draughtsman were put to good use and he sketched several reconnaissances, his sketches providing enough detail to compile a map.

It was for these skills that on Sunday, 1st June, Louis was selected to seek out a camp site for the 2nd Division. Lieutenant Carey sought permission to *accompany* the Prince, which was duly granted. An escort was furnished by six men of No. 3 Troop, Natal Horse (also known as Bettington's Horse, their commander being Captain R.A. Bettington). In addition six men of Captain T. Shepstone's Troop, Native Horse were ordered to join the party. At 9.15 a.m. the six men of the Natal Horse fell-in, together with a 'friendly' Zulu to act as a guide, but the Native troopers failed to report. Eager to get on with his task, Louis set off without awaiting their arrival. Brevet-Colonel Harrison saw the party on their patrol and suggested their numbers were insufficient, to which Louis replied, 'Oh no, we are quite strong enough.'

For hours the party went about their task, Louis sketched their surroundings, seeking an appropriate camp site. At 3 p.m. the party rode into a Zulu kraal, close to the banks of the Ityotyozi River. The kraal was deserted, but showed signs of recent habitation. Louis gave orders for the men to off-saddle their horses and allow them to feed. Their Zulu guide was despatched to fetch water so that the men could have some coffee and Louis lay down beside a hut to rest. No guard was posted.

At about 3.40 p.m. the native guide reported seeing a Zulu on an adjacent hill. The horses were gathered and saddled. Louis asked 'Are you all ready?' to which the troopers affirmed they were. The Prince then gave the order 'Prepare to mount'. If the next order was given it was drowned by a ragged volley emitted from the bush, out of which broke a number of Zulus (estimates of the strength of the Zulus vary from fifteen to forty men).

Trooper G. Rogers' horse bolted and, stranded on foot, he managed to loose off a shot from his carbine before falling to an assegai. Carey and the others rode towards the river. Trooper W. Abel fell from his mount, his flight stopped by a Martini Henry round in his back. As for the Prince, he struggled to mount his horse and his sword fell from its scabbard. He endeavoured to vault onto his horse, clinging to its saddle holster, but the leather tore, sending the Prince tumbling to the ground. Louis made off on foot, pursued by seven warriors. Gaining on their prey, one threw an assegai which struck Louis in the thigh. Louis plucked the spear from his leg and drawing his revolver fired two shots, neither of which found a mark. A flung assegai entered Louis' left shoulder and eventually he slumped to his knees. The Zulus closed in on him and he died under a flurry of assegai blades. The time was shortly before 4 p.m. Hopelessly outnumbered, Carey and the others had fled.

Composition of the British Force

His Imperial Highness, E.L.J.J.N. Bonaparte, no military rank, attached to Lieutenant-General Chelmsford's staff, commanding: Lieutenant J.B. Carey, 98th (The Prince of Wales') Regiment of Foot, DAQMG Lieutenant-General's staff

No. 3 Troop, Natal Horse
Sergeant R. Willis
Corporal J. Grubb
Troopers: W. Abel; Cochrane; Le Tocq; G. Rogers

HIS IMPERIAL HIGHNESS
E.L.J.J.N. BONAPARTE,
EXILED PRINCE IMPERIAL
OF FRANCE

LIEUTENANT
J.B. CAREY,
98TH FOOT

160

Guide
One 'friendly' Zulu

British and Colonial Casualties

KILLED IN ACTION
Staff: His Imperial Highness E.L.J.J.N. Bonaparte

No. 3 Troop, Natal Horse
Troopers: W. Abel; G. Rogers

Guide
One 'friendly' Zulu

Postscript
Someone had to pay the price for the death of the Prince Imperial. There was an obvious scapegoat, Lieutenant J.B. Carey. A court martial was hastily convened: its verdict was a foregone conclusion. Carey was found guilty on the charge of misbehaviour before the enemy. The court implied that Carey had command of the party, but as is apparent from the preceding text The Prince Imperial was responsible for issuing all orders to the detachment on that fateful day.

Carey returned to England where the liberal press had taken up his cause. Even Louis' mother, the Empress Eugénie, pleaded with Queen Victoria for clemency. The finding of the court was quashed and Carey allowed to return to his regiment.

He died in India in 1883 still bearing the stigma of that fateful June day in Zululand.

XII

The Reconnaissance across the
White Mfolozi River
Thursday, 3rd July 1879

'First Spear By Jove!' – *Captain Lord W.L. de la P.
Beresford, 9th Lancers*

LORD CHELMSFORD'S forces advanced into Zululand, towards King Cetshwayo's capital, Ulundi. Chelmsford was
determined to crush the Zulu defiance, to rid himself of the
stain of the disaster of Isandlwana and the death of the Prince
Imperial. King Cetshwayo, aware of the threat, attempted a
negotiated settlement. He sent emissaries to parley with
Chelmsford, who were received on 4th June at the encampment of the recently promoted Brigadier-General H.E. Wood's
'Flying Column' on the Nondweni.

Chelmsford did no more than dismiss the emissaries'
advances however; instead he dictated the following peace
terms to them:

1. The restoration of all captured cattle at Ulundi, together
   with the two cannon lost at Isandlwana.

2. A promise to be given by Cetshwayo that all arms taken
   during the war should be collected and surrendered.

3. That one Zulu regiment, to be nominated by Chelmsford,
   should come under a flag of truce and lay down its arms at a
   distance of one thousand yards from the British lines.

Other events began to determine Chelmsford's strategy. On
16th June he received information that he had been superseded

by Lieutenant-General Sir Garnet Wolseley. Fearful that he would be robbed of his chance to defeat the Zulu, Chelmsford advanced on Ulundi accompanying Major-General E. Newdigate's IInd Division and Wood's 'Flying Column'. King Cetshwayo, aware of the threat, ordered the remnants of the Zulu army to muster at Ulundi.

Chelmsford's advance was relentless. Many kraals in the line of advance were put to the torch and cattle taken as prizes. To hinder the advance, Zulus began firing the grass before the columns in an effort to destroy the forage required for the horses and oxen. Both armies were now waging a scorched earth policy. Despite the British aggression, Cetshwayo still attempted to negotiate a settlement and two further Zulu peace missions were received by Chelmsford on 27th and 30th June. Chelmsford modified his previous demands in that he was prepared to accept the return of 1,000 rifles taken at Isandlwana, in lieu of the surrender of a Zulu regiment. He announced his intention of moving towards the banks of the White Mfolozi River, but promised not to cross the river until after noon on Thursday, 3rd July, thereby giving time for his conditions to be fulfilled. He added that if the Zulu did not hinder his advance his forces would burn no further kraals.

On Tuesday, 1st July, the two British columns laagered on the southern bank of the White Mfolozi. The following day a small stone fort was constructed. Watering and bathing parties were detailed off to make use of the facilities the Mfolozi offered: during the advance there had been a scarcity of fresh water. Whilst indulging in this dubious pleasure (the river was infested with crocodiles) the details came under Zulu rifle fire and the British scampered for cover and returned the fire. At least one Zulu was wounded in the exchange.

King Cetshwayo attempted one last peace proposal: he was willing to give up at least 100 of his own cattle herd as a symbol of his submission. His attempt was foiled by the umCijo regiment who turned back the herd. His attempt thwarted, he addressed his gathered army. He told them that if they were to fight they were not to attempt to assault the British in their entrenched positions but rather to fight them in the open whilst on the move.

On Thursday, 3rd July, the water parties came under rifle fire from the northern shores. A company of the re-formed 1st Battalion, 24th Regiment of Foot, responded to the fire. Chelmsford's ultimatum expired at noon and as he had received no satisfactory reply to his demands he ordered a mounted reconnaissance to be conducted by a force commanded by Brevet Lieutenant-Colonel R.H. Buller. The purpose of the sortie was firstly to disperse the Zulu riflemen on the north bank, secondly to survey the land and select an appropriate site to fight the Zulu, and thirdly to provoke a Zulu attack in an effort to ascertain the strength and disposition of the Zulu force.

Buller led his force of just under 500 mounted men out at about 1.30 p.m. As a distraction two 9-pounder artillery pieces played on the Zulu hidden on the bluff. Commandant F.J. Baker led his men across the Mfolozi at a wagon drift slightly up-river from where Buller and the remainder of the force forded.

Baker's Horse quickly dislodged some thirty Zulus who scattered before the irregular horsemen. Baker perceived that there were a number of the enemy gathering on the surrounding hills and he despatched some gallopers to warn Buller, whose men were advancing at a cracking pace across the Mahlabathini Plain towards Ulundi in pursuit of a small party of Zulu. Lord William Beresford, 9th Lancers, who had gained leave of absence from his duties as aide-de-camp to the Viceroy of India, ran a Zulu through with his sword and exulted with the pig-sticking cry of, 'First spear by Jove!'

Buller ordered Commandant P.J. Raaf and his Transvaal Rangers to halt near to the kraal of kwaNodwengu, whilst the remaining troops continued after the fleeing Zulu. Buller, however, was blissfully unaware that these Zulus were merely a bait and he was leading his men into a classic box ambush. Lured on by other Zulu decoys, he was about to fall into the elaborate trap when he suddenly sensed all was not well and

THE ADVANCE OF MAJOR-GENERAL NEWDIGATE'S IIND
DIVISION TOWARDS THE ZULU CAPITAL, ULUNDI

MEN OF THE 17TH LANCERS DESTROYING
A KRAAL ON THE ADVANCE TO ULUNDI

THE EXCHANGE OF FIRE ACROSS THE WHITE MFOLOZI RIVER.
NOTE THE TELL-TALE SMOKE OF THE ZULU RIFLEMEN ON THE HILL
ON THE OPPOSITE BANK.

'FIRST SPEAR BY JOVE!'. CAPTAIN LORD W.L.
DE LA P. BERESFORD RUNNING THROUGH A ZULU.

called a halt. The Zulus enfiladed the horsemen with rifle fire, but fortunately their aim was poor and only four men dropped from their saddles. Two men had died instantly, the other two men were wounded and unhorsed and the Zulus were closing on them. Beresford and Sergeant E. O'Toole of the Frontier Light Horse managed with extreme difficulty to extricate Sergeant J. Fitzmaurice (or in some accounts Fitzmorris) of the 1st Battalion, 24th Regiment of Foot attached to 1st Squadron Mounted Infantry. Captain H.C.D. D'Arcy of the Frontier

CAPTAIN LORD
W.L. DE LA P. BERESFORD,
9TH LANCERS

Light Horse attempted to rescue Lance-Corporal J.A. Raubenheim of the same corps, but his horse bucked them off. D'Arcy managed to remount but due to a back injury he had sustained in the fall he was unable to heave up Raubenheim. With great reluctance D'Arcy was forced to abandon him to his fate.

Pressed by some 3,000 Zulu, Buller fell back on Raaf's position using fire and movement. In turn they retired on Baker's position; with rifle and artillery support from the southern bank the horsemen reached the British position.

Composition of the British Force

Brevet Lieutenant-Colonel R.H. Buller vc, cb, **60th Rifles (King's Royal Rifle Corps)** commanding:

Staff: Captain Lord W.L. de la P. Beresford, 9th Lancers, staff officer; Captain Sir T.G. Fermor-Hesketh, 2nd Royal Lancashire Militia, aide-de-camp

1st Squadron Mounted Infantry
Commanded by Lieutenant E.S. Browne, vc, 1st Battalion, 24th (2nd Warwickshires) Regiment of Foot
Captain F.M.G. Hutchinson, 2nd Battalion, 4th (King's Own) Regiment of Foot
Lieutenants: N. Newnham-Davis, 2nd Battalion, 3rd (East Kent) Regiment of Foot ('The Buffs'); H.A. Walsh, 1st Battalion, 13th (Somerset) Light Infantry
and 65 other ranks

Transvaal Rangers
Comprising five officers and 63 other ranks, commanded by Commandant P.J. Raaf

Frontier Light Horse
Comprising ten officers and 99 other ranks, commanded by Captain H.C.D. D'Arcy

Baker's Horse
Comprising six officers and 86 other ranks, commanded by Commandant F.J. Baker

Natal Light Horse
Comprising three officers and 56 other ranks, commanded by Commandant W.H. Whalley

Edendale Troop, Natal Native Horse
Comprising three officers and 89 other ranks, commanded by Lieutenant W.F.D. Cochrane, 32nd (Cornwall) Light Infantry

British and Colonial Casualties

KILLED IN ACTION
Frontier Light Horse
Trooper G. Pearce

Natal Light Horse
Private G. Peacock

MISSING IN ACTION (taken prisoner)
Frontier Light Horse
Lance-Corporal J.A. Raubenheim
(Raubenheim was alive when taken prisoner, although wounded. He was subsequently tortured to death during the night of 3rd/4th July 1879.)

WOUNDED IN ACTION
1st Squadron Mounted Infantry
(Listed by parent unit)

CAPTAIN H.C.D. D'ARCY,
FRONTIER LIGHT HORSE

1st Battalion, 24th (2nd Warwickshires) Regiment of Foot
Sergeant J. Fitzmaurice (or Fitzmorris), severely wounded

Frontier Light Horse
Trooper J. Tracy, severely wounded

Natal Light Horse
Private A. Kantz, dangerously wounded

Transvaal Rangers
Trooper E. Meyles, dangerously wounded

HONOURS AND AWARDS

The Victoria Cross
Captain Lord William BERESFORD, 9th Lancers
The London Gazette
9th September 1879
For gallant conduct in having at great personal risk, during the retirement of the reconnoitring party across the 'White Umvolosi River' on 3rd July last, turned to assist Sergeant Fitzmaurice, 1st Battalion, 24th Foot (whose horse had fallen with him) mounted him behind him on his horse, and brought him away to safety under the close fire of the Zulus who were in great force, and coming on quickly.

Lord William Beresford's position was rendered most dangerous from the fact that Sergeant Fitzmaurice twice nearly pulled him from his horse.

*

Captain (now Commandant) Cecil D'ARCY, Frontier Light Horse
The London Gazette
10th October 1879
For his gallant conduct on the 3rd July 1879 during the reconnaissance made before Ulundi by the Mounted Corps, in endeavouring to rescue Trooper Raubenheim of the Frontier Light Horse, who fell from his horse as the troops were retiring. Captain D'Arcy, though the Zulus were close upon them, waited for the man to mount behind him; the horse kicked them both off, and though much hurt by the fall and quite alone, Captain D'Arcy coolly endeavoured to lift the trooper, who was stunned, on to the horse, and it was only when he found that he had no strength to do so that he mounted and rode off.

His escape was miraculous as the Zulus had actually closed upon him.

*

Sergeant Edmund O'TOOLE, Frontier Light Horse
The London Gazette
10th October 1879
For his conspicuous courage and bravery on several occasions during the campaign, and especially for his conduct on the 3rd July 1879, at the close of the reconnaissance before Ulundi, in assisting to rescue

Sergeant Fitzmaurice, 1st Battalion, 24th Mounted Infantry, whose horse fell and rolled on him as the troops retired before great numbers of the enemy. When lifted up behind him by Lord William Beresford, the man, being half stunned by the fall, could not hold on, and he must have been left had not Sergeant O'Toole, who was keeping back the advancing Zulus, given up his carbine and assisted to hold Sergeant Fitzmaurice on the horse. At the time the Zulus were rapidly closing on them, and there was no armed man between them and Sergeant O'Toole.

The Silver Medal for Distinguished Conduct in the Field

Corps	*Name*	*Date of Submission*
Edendale Troop, Natal Native Horse	Troop Sergeant-Major S. Kambula	Sept 1879

XIII

The Battle of Ulundi
Friday, 4th July 1879

'Steady my lads; close up, fire low and not so fast!' –
Brigadier-General H.E. Wood, VC

CHELMSFORD WAS aware that he must defeat the Zulu before Wolseley assumed command in the field, and from the intelligence gleaned from Buller's reconnaissance, he knew he had to make his move now. At about 6 a.m. on 4th July, Buller led his mounted men across the White Mfolozi by the lower drift and took up position on the bluff which commanded the upper drift.

There was bitterness in the camp on the south bank of the Mfolozi. Someone had to remain and guard the encampment and the duty rosters dealt a cruel blow: the task fell to the reconstructed 1st Battalion, 24th Regiment of Foot, the men who most wanted to avenge the massacre of Isandlwana would be denied their chance.

Wood's 'Flying Column' crossed first, and the IInd Division completed their crossing shortly after 7 a.m. The task was unopposed. The troops laboured through dense undergrowth before reaching the open country off the Mahlabathini Plain. Buller's irregular horsemen scouted ahead in the direction of kwaNodwengu. Whilst Wood's command halted and began forming the front of the square, Newdigate's men completed the formation. Chelmsford had formed a living laager from his infantrymen; twelve artillery pieces and two Gatling guns added to the fire power. Within the hollow square (or to be more accurate a hollow rectangle) were a company of Royal

Engineers; reserve infantry companies; a field hospital; ammunition wagons; a battalion of Natal Native Contingent; and a contingent of Wood's Irregulars. Outside the formation, the front and both flanks, ranged Buller's irregular horsemen. Forming the rear guard were two squadrons of the 17th Lancers and a troop of Native Horse.

The appearance of the square was somewhat cumbersome at first but Chelmsford marshalled the formation into a semblance of order. The band of the 13th Light Infantry struck up martial airs, the colours of the regiments were uncased, and the formation advanced across the Mahlabathini Plain. As the rear guard passed the kraal of kwaBulawayo the Native Horse put it to the torch. The square moved on, passing the kraal of kwaNodwengu. This almost suffered the same fate as kwaBulawayo but as the dense smoke rolled along the ground from the burning huts, Chelmsford realised it provided a perfect screen for the enemy and ordered it to be extinguished.

Buller's irregular horsemen retraced their steps from the previous day. The Zulus skirted them, hanging back. Anxious to engage the enemy Buller sent forward a small detachment of Baker's Horse, commanded by Lieutenant Parminter, to provoke the Zulus into attacking. Galled by the gesture, the Zulus rushed the party and attempted to cut them off, but Parminter managed to extricate his men without loss.

Chelmsford had by now halted the square, and the regular cavalry withdrew into the formation. At opposite sides of the square, the right front and the rear left, the Natal Native Horse troops, commanded by Lieutenant W.F.D. Cochrane and Captain T. Shepstone respectively, chided the Zulu, endeavouring to provoke an attack. Slowly they withdrew into the comparative safety of the square.

The Zulu encircled the square and the artillery pieces crashed into action at about 8.45 a.m. The infantry were ranked four deep, the front two ranks kneeling, the rear standing. As the Zulu closed every face of the square became engaged. The artillery pounded the oncoming warriors, whilst the Gatlings clawed into the Zulu ranks. Wood urged his

infantry: 'Steady my lads; close up, fire low, and not so fast!'
The Zulu responded with inaccurate rifle fire and very few
casualties were sustained.

Those within the square who had witnessed Zulu attacks in
previous engagements felt the assault lacked the ardour, the
ferocity of previous actions. There was a determined rush from
the direction of kwaNodwengu of some 2,000 to 3,000 warriors on the corner of the square held by the 21st and 58th
Regiments of Foot. Lord Chelmsford, seeing the emergency,
implored the men, 'Cannot you fire faster?'. The infantry
obliged, their concentrated fire destroying the Zulu attack.

Colonel D.C. Drury Lowe, 17th Lancers, was struck from
his horse, having been hit by a spent round. He made a brief
self-examination and satisfied he had sustained no serious
injury he remounted. Drury Lowe had served in the Crimea,
but he had not ridden in the Charge of the Light Brigade,
although his brother had. A wound would not rob him of the
chance to participate in the cavalry charge.

The Zulu attacks were now faltering all round. They fell
back, disorganised by the effect of the British firepower.
Chelmsford unleashed his regular cavalry, 'Go at them, Lowe,
but don't pursue too far!'. Drury Lowe led his squadrons out
of the rear face of the square, formed and charged the fleeing
Zulu. From the front of the square issued Buller's horsemen, a
troop of the King's Dragoon Guards and the Mounted Infantry. A relentless, pitiless pursuit commenced with no quarter
being sought by the Zulu and certainly none being offered by
the British. There were scores to settle, Isandlwana to be
avenged. Clemency was thrown to the wind as the Native
Horse and Contingent set about butchering the Zulu wounded
to a man. The kraals which dotted the plain were put to the
torch. The cannon pounded the retiring Zulu, then the gunners
turned their attention on shelling Ulundi.

Shortly after 10 a.m. Chelmsford ordered Buller to burn
Ulundi. A race commenced to see who would be there first and
was won by 'Bill' Beresford. The Zulu capital was set aflame,
the fires of its destruction would burn for days. As for King

SWAZI WARRIORS OF COMMANDANT T. LORAINE WHITE'S
BATTALION OF WOOD'S IRREGULARS ON THE MARCH

ZULU WARRIORS MUSTERING FOR AN ATTACK. THE THREE WARRIORS ON THE

IGHT ARE PRESUMABLY MEANT TO DEPICT IZINDUNA, I.E. MILITARY COMMANDERS.

1, The 90th Regiment.   2, Companies of 80th Regiment.   3, Two guns.   4, Brigadier-General Sir Evelyn Wood.   5, The Lancers waiting   6, Two Gatling guns.   7, The 13th Regiment.
14, Ammunition-cart.   15, Dragoons kneeling, holding their horses.   16, Wounded man brought in, surgeon beside him.   17, Dragoon and horse just killed.   18, Bengough's Natives, h

INSIDE THE SQUARE AT THE BATTLE OF ULUNDI, FRIDAY, 4TH JULY 1879. LORD
LEFT, IS BEING BORNE BY TWO NATIVE HOSPITAL-BEARERS TO THE FIELD HOSPITAL
BEING CARRIED BY TWO OTHER RANKS OF THE

, which jumped 2 ft. in the air.   9, Ammunition-cart.   10, Staff officer giving instructions.   11, Hospital water-cart.   12, Hospital, with surgeons at work.   13, Lord Chelmsford and staff.
st.   19, Wounded officer assisted to the centre, or to the hospital.   20, Carrying ammunition to 21st Regiment.   21, Dragoons.   22, Bullock in ammunition-cart just killed.   23, Ulundi.

HELMSFORD IS DEPICTED CENTRE RIGHT, MOUNTED ON A PALE HORSE. A CASUALTY,
ENTRE MIDDLE, DENOTED BY THE CROSS OF GENEVA. NOTE THE AMMUNITION BOX
1ST ROYAL SCOTS FUSILIERS TO THE FIRING-LINE.

THE CHARGE OF THE 17TH LANCERS AT ULUNDI

THE WAR ARTIST C.E. FRIPP SKETCHES THE ZULU DEAD AT ULUNDI,
A SAD TESTIMONY TO THE FEROCITY OF THE BRITISH FIREPOWER.

CASUALTIES BEING BORNE AWAY ON 'DHOOLIES', I.E. SHELTERED STRETCHERS. AS BRITISH TROOPS LOOK ON, ULUNDI AND THE NEIGHBOURING KRAALS BURN. THE ENGRAVING DEPICTS AT LEAST TWO SOLDIERS WITH ASSEGAIS EVIDENTLY TAKEN AS THE SPOILS OF WAR.

Cetshwayo, he had fled Ulundi on the 3rd, and had been sheltering at a nearby kraal. Now, with his army defeated, he too fled, a fugitive in his own kingdom.

The last battle of the Anglo-Zulu War had been fought.

Composition of the British Force

Lieutenant-General Lord Chelmsford commanding:
Personal Staff: Brevet Lieutenant-Colonel J.N. Crealock, 95th (Der-

MAJOR-GENERAL E. NEWDIGATE

byshire) Regiment of Foot, Military Secretary; Captain W.C.F. Molyneux, 22nd (Cheshire) Regiment of Foot and Lieutenant A.B. Milne, HMS *Active*, aides-de-camp; Brevet Colonel R. Harrison, Royal Engineers, Quartermaster-General; Lieutenant-Colonel C.J. East (Half-pay), formerly 57th (West Middlesex) Regiment of Foot, Deputy Quartermaster-General; Major F.W. Grenfell, 60th Rifles (King's Royal Rifle Corps), Deputy Assistant Adjutant-General; The Honourable W. Drummond, Head of the Intelligence Department; Lieutenant-Colonel J.T.B. Brown, Royal Artillery, Commanding Artillery; Captain J. Allenye, Royal Artillery, adjutant to R.A. Commander

185

IInd DIVISION
Major-General E. Newdigate commanding
Staff: Captain R.B. Lane, Rifle Brigade, aide-de-camp; Lieutenant &
   Captain Sir W.G. Gordon-Cumming, Scots Guards, staff officer;
   Lieutenant & Captain the Honourable R.S.G.S. Cotton, Scots
   Guards, orderly officer; Major C.W. Robinson, Rifle Brigade,
   Assistant Adjutant-General; Brevet Major F.S. Russell, 14th
   (King's) Hussars, Deputy Assistant Adjutant-General; Major
   M.W.E. Gossett, 54th (West Norfolk) Regiment of Foot, Assistant
   Quartermaster-General; Captain W.E. Montgomery, Scots
   Guards, Deputy Assistant Quartermaster-General; Major R. Ale-
   xander, Royal Artillery, commanding the ammunition column;
   Brevet Major E. Essex, 75th (Stirlingshire) Regiment of Foot,
   Director of Transport; Deputy Commissary J.A. Boyd, Commis-
   sariat and Transport Department; Deputy-Assistant Commissary-
   General of Ordnance J. Steevens, Ordnance Store Department;
   Major H.S. Stabb, 32nd (Cornwall) Light Infantry; Lieutenant
   W.L. Davidson, Royal Artillery; Captain T.H. Anstey, Royal
   Engineers

CAVALRY DETACHMENT
Commanded by Colonel D.C. Drury-Lowe, formerly of 17th (Duke
   of Cambridge's Own) Lancers, comprising:

1st (King's) Dragoon Guards
Brevet Major W.V. Brownlow (also performing duties as Assistant
   Transport Officer and extra aide-de-camp to Colonel Drury-
   Lowe); Lieutenant R.A.B. French-Brewster (acting as Deputy
   Provost-Marshal); and 24 other ranks

17th (Duke of Cambridge's Own) Lancers
Major S. Boulderson
Captains: J.C. Duke; T.A. Cooke; The Hon E.V. Wyatt-Edgell; E.A.
   Belford; J.F. Alexander; The Hon J. Pleydell-Bouverie; W.T.S.
   Kevill-Davies; C.E. Swaine
Lieutenants: G.A. Wood; M.G. Neeld; H.C. Jenkins; C.H. Purvis;
   E.B. Herbert; The Hon L.H.D. Fortescue
Second-Lieutenants: C.J. Anstruther Thomas and C.H. Butler
Quartermaster J. Berryman, VC
Veterinary Surgeons: J. Lambert and G.J.R. Rayment

186

COLONEL
D.C. DRURY-LOWE,
COMMANDER OF THE
CAVALRY DETACHMENT

LIEUTENANT VISCOUNT
ST. VINCENT

Attached Personnel
Lieutenant Viscount St Vincent, 7th Hussars
Lieutenant W.C. James, 2nd Dragoons (Scots Greys)
Lieutenant Lord H.G. Beaumont, 1st West Yorkshire Yeomanry
and 285 other ranks

Royal Artillery
'N' Battery, 5th Brigade
Brevet Lieutenant-Colonel A. Harness
Lieutenant C.S.B. Parsons

'N' Battery, 6th Brigade
Major F.T. Le Grice
Captain N.N. Crookenden
Lieutenants: E.H. Elliot; F.J.A. Trench; J. Wodehouse
Veterinary Surgeon W. Hagger
and 140 other ranks drawn from both batteries, serving six 9-
   pounder cannon and two 7-pounder cannon

INFANTRY BRIGADE
Colonel R.T. Glyn, 1st Battalion, 24th (2nd Warwickshires) Regi-
   ment of Foot commanding:
Staff: Captain W.L. Dalrymple, 88th (Connaught Rangers) Regi-
   ment of Foot, Brigade Major; Lieutenants A.B. Phipps, 2nd
   Battalion, 24th (2nd Warwickshires) Regiment of Foot and G.E.
   Liebenrood, 58th (Rutlandshire) Regiment of Foot

2nd Battalion, 21st Royal Scots Fusiliers
Brevet Lieutenant-Colonel A.G. Hazelrigg commanding:
Major R.W.C. Winsloe
Captains: C.B. Robinson; J.M. Gordon; D. Auchinleck
Lieutenants: F.R.H. Lambart; P.W. Browne; W.A. Young
Second-Lieutenants: The Hon A.S. Hardinge; H.S. McC. Stannell
Quartermaster J. Clifford

Attached Personnel
Lieutenant H. Higgins, 3rd Royal Lancashire Militia
and 203 other ranks

58th (Rutlandshire) Regiment of Foot
Lieutenant-Colonel R.C. Whitehead commanding:
Majors: W.D. Bond; W.H. Hingeston; J.V. Hesse

LIEUTENANT
F.R.H. LAMBART,
2ND/21ST FUSILIERS

MAJOR
W.H. HINGESTON,
58TH FOOT

189

Brevet Major D.G. Anderson
Captains: O.B. St. John; A.W. Morris; E. Lovegrove; H.M. Nuthall
Lieutenants: H. Dolphin; E. Del Sandys; T.E. Compton
Second-Lieutenants: W.F. Fawcett; J. Collinson; H. Morgan; A.C.
  Bolton
Quartermaster C. Lenton
and 407 other ranks

94th Regiment of Foot
Lieutenant-Colonel S. Malthus commanding:

LIEUTENANT
J. MACSWINEY,
94TH FOOT

Brevet Lieutenant-Colonel J. Murray
Major P.R. Anstruther
Captains: J. Browne; F.B. Campbell; S.N. M'L. Nairne; E.S. Brook;
  L.G. Brooke; H.W.W. Spooner
Lieutenants: H.F.G. Campion; J. MacSwiney; H.A.C. Harrison; J.
  de C. O'Grady
Second-Lieutenants: G.L.E. Massy; J.J.F. Hume
Captain and Paymaster J.M. Elliot
Quartermaster P. Lacey
and 616 other ranks

190

LIEUTENANT
H.A.C. HARRISON,
94TH FOOT

CAPTAIN
AND PAYMASTER
J.M. ELLIOT,
94TH FOOT

191

The following Imperial officers were also present, apparently un-attached to any specific duties:

Grenadier Guards
Lieutenants: The Hon R.C.G. Carington; The Hon C.R.W. Colville

Coldstream Guards
Lieutenant and Captain The Hon G.A.V. Bertie

1st Battalion, 24th (2nd Warwickshires) Regiment of Foot
Majors: W.M. Brander; J.M.G. Tongue

VOLUNTEER SURGEON
D. GLANVILLE

Captain T. Rainforth
Lieutenants: W. Heaton; R.A.P. Clements
Second Lieutenant W.W. Lloyd

2nd Battalion, 24th (2nd Warwickshires) Regiment of Foot
Major W.M. Dunbar
Captain L.H. Bennett

2nd Regiment, Natal Native Contingent
Major H.M. Bengough, 77th (East Middlesex) Regiment of Foot
   commanding 404 all ranks, native and European

Shepstone's Native Horse
Captain T. Shepstone commanding 118 all ranks, native and European

No. 3 Troop, Natal Horse
Twelve other ranks

Field Hospital
Medical staff from both columns

Army Medical Department
Surgeon-Majors: F.B. Scott; P.W. Stafford; J.A. Anderson; J.H. Reynolds, VC; J. O'Reilly; A.L. Browne
Surgeon: R.V. Ash

VOLUNTEER SURGEON
P.B. CONOLLY. A LATER
PICTURE, CIRCA 1884.

Volunteer Surgeons: D. Glanville; P.B. Conolly
Civilian Surgeons: Dr A.R. Busby; Dr D. Blair Brown
and two other unidentified officers/doctors

Army Hospital Corps
Lieutenant of Orderlies W. Pike
and 21 other ranks and 91 native hospital bearers

Chaplains' Department
Chaplain The Rev C.J. Coar, MA
Temporary Chaplain The Rev G. Smith

FLYING COLUMN
Brevet Brigadier-General H.E. Wood, vc commanding:
Staff: Lieutenant H. Lysons, 90th (Perthshire Volunteers) Light
Infantry, Orderly Officer; Commissary E. Hughes, Commissariat
and Transport Department, Acting Orderly Officer; Major F.C.
Clery (Half-Pay) formerly 32nd (Cornwall) Light Infantry, Prin-
cipal Staff Officer; Captain E.R.P. Woodgate, 4th (King's Own)
Regiment of Foot, Assistant Adjutant General; Deputy Commis-
saries G. Coates and W.A. Dunne, Commissariat and Transport
Department; Deputy Assistant Commissary C.G.L. Campbell,
Ordnance Store Department; Captain H. Vaughan, Royal Artil-
lery; Major C.J. Moysey, Royal Engineers

Royal Artillery
10th Battery, 7th Brigade (Gatling gun battery)
Major J.F. Owen
Lieutenant H.M.L. Rundle

11th Battery, 7th Brigade
Major E.G. Tremlett
Brevet Major H.R.Y. Browne
Lieutenant F.G. Slade
and 80 other ranks of both Batteries serving two Gatling guns and
four 7-pounder cannon

5th (Field) Company, Royal Engineers
Brevet Major W.P. Jones commanding:
Brevet Major J.R.M. Chard, vc
Lieutenants: R. da C. Porter; C.E. Commeline; T.R. Main (attached)
and 62 other ranks (including attached)

1st Battalion, 13th (Somerset) Light Infantry
Major E.J. England commanding:
Captains: J.F. James; D.T. Perssé; G.H.A. Kinloch; W.H. Evans;
W.H.H. Thurlow; J.M.E. Waddy; R.C. Otway; E.J. Fownes; E.J.
Gallwey
Lieutenants: F.J. Justice; E.W. Clark; E.M. Poyton; R. Levinge; R.B.
Williams; A.W.A. Pollock; R.L. Payne; J.C. Allen; G.A. Pardoe
Second-Lieutenants: J.W.H. West; R.W.G. Hillias
and 587 other ranks

80th (Staffordshire Volunteers) Regiment of Foot
Major C. Tucker commanding:
Captains: W.T. Anderson; J.E.H. Prior; H.J. Anderson; J.O. Sherrard; L.C. Potts
Lieutenants: T.J. Chamberlain; A.W. Hast; A.H. Lindop; E.K. Daubeney; B.W.R. Ussher
and 357 other ranks

90th (Perthshire Volunteers) Light Infantry
Major R.M. Rogers, VC, commanding:
Major A. Cherry
Captains: W.S. Hamilton; W.F. Wilson; R. Lawrence; A.B. Maude; G.W. Hutchinson; G.R. Heathcote; J.H. Laye
Lieutenants: S.H. Lomax; H.M. Campbell; A. Gordon; S.P. Strong; H.E. Hotham; A.O. White; J. Ross; C.M.I. Hopkins
Paymaster F. Taylor
Quartermaster J. Newman
and 688 other ranks

Wood's Irregulars
Commandant T. Loraine White commanding 336 all ranks

Natal Native Pioneers
Captain J. Nolan commanding 50 all ranks

Mounted Troops
Brevet Lieutenant-Colonel R.H. Buller, VC, CB, 60th Rifles (King's Royal Rifle Corps) commanding:
Staff: Captain Lord W.L. de la P. Beresford, 9th Lancers, staff officer; Captain Sir T.G. Fermor-Hesketh, 2nd Royal Lancashire Militia, aide-de-camp

1st Squadron Mounted Infantry
Lieutenant E.S. Browne, VC, 1st Battalion, 24th (2nd Warwickshires) Regiment of Foot commanding:
Captain F.M.G. Hutchinson, 2nd Battalion, 4th (King's Own) Regiment of Foot
Lieutenants: N. Newnham-Davis, 2nd Battalion, 3rd (East Kent) Regiment of Foot ('The Buffs'); H.A. Walsh, 1st Battalion, 13th (Somerset) Light Infantry
and 64 other ranks

Transvaal Rangers
Comprising five officers and 62 other ranks, commanded by Commandant P.J. Raaf

Frontier Light Horse
Comprising ten officers and 96 other ranks, under the nominal command of Captain H.C.D. D'Arcy

Baker's Horse
Comprising six officers and 86 other ranks, commanded by Commandant F.J. Baker

Natal Light Horse
Comprising three officers and 54 other ranks, commanded by Commandant W.H. Whalley

Edendale Troop, Natal Native Horse
Comprising three officers and 89 other ranks, commanded by Lieutenant W.F.D. Cochrane, 32nd (Cornwall) Light Infantry

British and Colonial Casualties

KILLED IN ACTION
IInd Division
17th (Duke of Cambridge's Own) Lancers
Captain the Hon E.V. Wyatt Edgell
Farrier-Sergeant J. Taylor

58th (Rutlandshire) Regiment of Foot
Lance-Corporal J. Tomkinson

94th Regiment of Foot
Privates: B. Coates; S. Kent

Shepstone's Native Horse
Troopers: K. Lopela; J. Mgadi; E. Tigingela; Tundu

Flying Column
11th Battery, 7th Brigade, Royal Artillery
Corporal C. Carter

13th (Somerset) Light Infantry
Private J. Bridley

80th (Staffordshire Volunteers) Regiment of Foot
Sergeant H. Watts
Private J. Floyd

Edendale Troop, Natal Native Horse
Trooper Jonas

MISSING IN ACTION (presumed dead)
Lieutenant-General's Staff
The Hon W. Drummond, body found on 18th August 1879

CAPTAIN THE HON.
E.V. WYATT EDGELL,
17TH LANCERS

WOUNDED IN ACTION
Lieutenant-General's Staff
HMS Active
Lieutenant A.B. Milne, slightly wounded
Signaller J.E.R. Gostling, severely wounded

IInd Division
Major-General Newdigate's Staff
Scots Guards
Lieutenant and Captain the Hon R.S.G.S. Cotton, slightly wounded

Royal Artillery
Lieutenant W.L. Davidson, slightly wounded

17th (Duke of Cambridge's Own) Lancers
Colonel D.C. Drury-Lowe, slightly wounded
Lieutenant H.C. Jenkins, severely wounded
Troopers: E. Jones, mortally wounded, died of wounds 4th July 1879; J. Keegan, slightly wounded; C. Waite, dangerously wounded

2nd Dragoons (Scots Greys) (Attached 17th Lancers)
Lieutenant W.C. James, slightly wounded

'N' Battery, 6th Brigade, Royal Artillery
Driver D. Brennan, severely wounded

Infantry Brigade
(Colonel Glyn's Staff)

2nd Battalion, 24th (2nd Warwickshires) Regiment of Foot
Lieutenant A.B. Phipps, severely wounded

58th (Rutlandshire) Regiment of Foot
Lieutenant G.E. Liebenrood, severely wounded (shot twice)

2nd Battalion, 21st Royal Scots Fusiliers
Brevet Lieutenant-Colonel A.G. Hazelrigg, severely wounded
Major R.W.C. Winsloe, severely wounded
Privates: J. Bevan, dangerously wounded; W. Bonner, dangerously wounded; G. Brown, severely wounded; H. Calder, dangerously wounded; J. Daveney, severely wounded; M. Dowdle, dangerously wounded; F. Fiddler, severely wounded; J. Hennessy, slightly wounded; P. McRae, slightly wounded

58th (Rutlandshire) Regiment of Foot
Major W.D. Bond, severely wounded
Colour-Sergeants: J. Piper, severely wounded; T. Wallingford, severely wounded
Drummer H. Stewart, dangerously wounded
Privates: J. Cotterell, severely wounded; W.J. Donnolly, slightly wounded; C. Fosh, dangerously wounded; J. Garrity, dangerously wounded (by friendly fire); H.W. Howie, severely wounded; W. Lacey, severely wounded; W. Maloney, dangerously wounded; M. Maroney, mortally wounded, died of wounds 12th July 1879;

W. Severett, severely wounded; W. Sergeant, dangerously wounded

94th Regiment of Foot
Captain L.G. Brooke, slightly wounded
Sergeants: J. McNally, severely wounded; R. Popple, severely wounded
Lance-Sergeant E. Hunt, dangerously wounded
Privates: H. Cotterill, dangerously wounded; A. Croxford, dangerously wounded; G. Godden, slightly wounded; T. Grimes, slightly wounded; M. Murhill, slightly wounded; P. Murtha, dangerously wounded; C. Penfold, mortally wounded, died of wounds 25th July 1879

2nd Regiment, Natal Native Contingent
Lieutenants: H. Lukin, slightly wounded; L.N. Moncrief, slightly wounded
Privates: Hea, severely wounded; Mori, severely wounded; Pender, slightly wounded; Tulman, dangerously wounded

Shepstone's Native Horse
Trooper Umzaaza, dangerously wounded

Field Hospital
Hospital Bearer Umbiquito, severely wounded

Flying Column
Royal Artillery
10th Battery, 7th Brigade
Bombardier J.R. Clarke, slightly wounded
Gunners: E. Dumpleton, slightly wounded; W. Moorhead, severely wounded; J. Morton, dangerously wounded

11th Battery, 7th Brigade
Gunner D. Rochford, mortally wounded. Died of wounds

7th Company, Royal Engineers (Attached 5th Company)
Sergeant R. Wood, severely wounded

1st Battalion, 13th (Somerset) Light Infantry
Lieutenant G.A. Pardoe, mortally wounded. Died of wounds 14th July 1879
Lance-Corporal C. Walker, slightly wounded

Buglers: J. Burns, mortally wounded. Died of wounds 4th July 1879.
M. Cockling, mortally wounded. Died of wounds 6th July 1879
Privates: J. Bourne, severely wounded; J. Davies, mortally wounded.
Died of wounds 6th July 1879. J. Duf, severely wounded; W. Hart,
severely wounded; C. Johnson, severely wounded; H. Owens,
severely wounded; J. Owing, severely wounded; W. Sheppard,
mortally wounded. Died of wounds 11th July 1879. W.G. Ship-
ton, dangerously wounded; T. Stokes, slightly wounded; J. Swain,
slightly wounded; A. Ward, severely wounded

LIEUTENANT
G.A. PARDOE,
1ST/13TH LIGHT
INFANTRY

80th (Staffordshire Volunteers) Regiment of Foot
Sergeant T. O'Neill, severely wounded
Privates: A. Beecroft, severely wounded; M. Duffy, severely wounded; W. Hunt, dangerously wounded; W. Lunt, dangerously
wounded; P. Tulley, severely wounded

90th (Perthshire Volunteers) Light Infantry
Sergeant W. Seaman, slightly wounded
Privates: J. Clifton, slightly wounded; J. Flood, severely wounded; J.
Green, slightly wounded; O. Kelly, slightly wounded; R. Landy,

severely wounded; W. McGuin, slightly wounded; P. Quinn, slightly wounded; W. Spearing, slightly wounded

Wood's Irregulars
Commandant T. Loraine White, slightly wounded
Captain S.S. Harber, severely wounded
Lieutenant E.J. Cowdell, severely wounded

Natal Native Pioneers
Lieutenants: F. Andrews, slightly wounded; H. Hickley, slightly wounded

ARCHIBALD FORBES,
OF THE 'DAILY NEWS'

1st Squadron Mounted Infantry
(Listed by parent unit)

1st Battalion, 24th (2nd Warwickshires) Regiment of Foot
Private J. Haley, slightly wounded

Baker's Horse
Troopers: P. Legge, severely wounded; P. Segos, severely wounded

Natal Light Horse
Corporal J. Farrell, severely wounded

Trooper H.E. Davis, mortally wounded. Died of wounds 4th July 1879

Edendale Troop, Natal Native Horse
Troopers: T. Kumalo, slightly wounded; Inyougan, slightly wounded; Salem, slightly wounded; Siagdo, dangerously wounded

War Correspondent Daily News
Mr A. Forbes, slightly wounded

Zulu Casualties

Approximately 1,500 killed or mortally wounded.

HONOURS AND AWARDS

The Silver Medal for Distinguished Conduct in the Field

Regiment	Name	Date of Submission
10th Battery 7th Brigade, Royal Artillery	Gunner W. Moorhead	1/6/1880
58th (Rutlandshire) Regiment of Foot	Colour Sergeant J. Phillips	21/6/1882

XIV

The Pursuit and Capture of King Cetshwayo
The End of the Zulu War

'I never thought troops could come down the
mountain through the forest . . .'
– King Cetshwayo kaMpande

WITH KING CETSHWAYO in flight and Ulundi in ashes,
Chelmsford was the master of the field. But it was a
mastery he soon relinquished. On the day following his victory
he acknowledged Wolseley's appointment and, without con-
solidating his position near to the Zulu capital, ordered a
withdrawal. On 15th July Wolseley and Chelmsford met at the
St Paul's Mission Station. There Chelmsford submitted his
resignation and began his return journey to Britain.

Despite the surrender of large numbers of coastal Zulus,
Wolseley was disquietened by the fact that a fugitive Cetshwayo could be seen as a rallying point by those inland and
northern Zulus who had not submitted. With re-organised
columns, Wolseley therefore advanced on Ulundi. Having
received information that a number of izinDuna wished to
surrender their forces at Ulundi on 10th August, he hastened
his advance to the ruined capital but to no end – he found no
submissive Zulus. On 11th August, a detachment still moving
towards Ulundi discovered the two 7-pounder cannon lost at
Isandlwana in a deserted kraal. They were brought into Ulundi
and placed at the base of the flagstaff outside Wolseley's tent.

Paramount in Wolseley's mind was the capture of Cetshwayo. Parties scoured the countryside hunting the refugee.
On 26th August information was received that Cetshwayo
was believed to be heading for the Ngome Forest. On the

following day Major R.J.C. Marter of the 1st (King's) Dragoon Guards set out with a force comprising a squadron of his regiment, a company of NNC, Lonsdale's Horse and ten mounted infantrymen. On the 28th, acting on information from an intercepted message intended for another search party, and with the assistance of two unwittingly duped Zulus, Marter was led to a summit overlooking the Ngome Forest. Peering down he saw in the deep valley, a small kraal nestling

MAJOR R.J.C. MARTER,
1ST DRAGOON GUARDS

near to a rocky stream, and it was here that Marter concluded the fugitive king was in hiding.

Marter ordered the NNC company, under a Captain Plesh, to descend the precipitous rock face whilst he led mounted men three miles northwards until he discovered a less hazardous face. Ordered to discard their sword scabbards and any unnecessary equipment, Plesh and his men descended to the valley floor while Marter formed his men and galloped towards the kraal. As the dragoons drew near, the NNC company sprang from hiding and dashed towards the huts shout-

THE TWO CANNON LOST BY 'N' BATTERY, 5TH BRIGADE, ROYAL ARTILLERY,
IN THE ACTION AT ISANDLWANA AND RECOVERED ON 11TH AUGUST 1879.

ZULU IZINDUNA SIGNING THE PEACE AGREEMENT, MONDAY, 1ST SEPTEMBER 1879

ing, 'The white men are here – you are taken!'. Major Marter called on Cetshwayo to surrender. The king, emerging from a hut accepted his fate – it was about 3.15 p.m. His small party of the king's retainers offered no resistance for they were too few in number – an inDuna named Mkhosana, nine men and a boy, five women and a girl. Marter's only casualty had been a trooper who had dislocated his elbow.

Cetshwayo was overheard to say to Mkhosana 'How did they get here?', to which Mkhosana pointed to the heights. The king added, 'I never thought troops could come down the mountain through the forest or I should not have been taken.'

Marter recovered from the kraal four Martini-Henry rifles and a bugle, all marked to the 24th Regiment of Foot, apparently spoils taken at Isandlwana. At 3.45 p.m. Marter and his heavily guarded charge struck out for Ulundi but their progress was slow. By nightfall they had only gone five miles. Starting at daybreak on the 29th, the prisoner and his escort progressed some twelve miles when, at 11 a.m., they encountered another search party, led by Captain Lord Gifford, VC, of the 57th (West Middlesex) Regiment of Foot. Gifford had been robbed of the chance of the capture of Cetshwayo by less than five hours. He had bided his time and intended to storm the kraal where Marter had seized the king at 8 p.m. Gifford and his party now made for Ulundi to convey Marter's report.

As evening fell the party were in 'Indian file' due to the rocky terrain and their passing through dense bush. Three men and a woman of the king's party, who had been feigning tiredness and extending the line, suddenly dashed to the cover of the bush to escape. Two of the men fell in the fire of the escort, the other man, apparently the king's snuff box carrier, and the woman escaped. That night the escort was reinforced by two companies of the 3rd Battalion, 60th Rifles (King's Royal Rifle Corps).

On the morning of Sunday, 31st August, King Cetshwayo re-entered his capital, Ulundi. Marter noticed his depressed expression as he surveyed the ruins, but he quickly cast off his dejection and marched regally into the custody of Sir Garnet

Wolseley. Within hours he was despatched under escort on a journey which would conclude in Cape Town, where he would enter into exile.

On the following day, Monday, 1st September 1879, Wolseley announced to the izinDuna, who had begun to gather at Ulundi to surrender, his plans for the fate of Zululand. The kingdom was to be divided into thirteen separate districts, each presided over by its own chief. The izinDuna witnessed and put their marks to an agreement which ran thus:

KING CETSHWAYO,
IN EUROPEAN DRESS
WHILST IN
CAPTIVITY

I recognise the victory of the British arms over the Zulu nation, and the full right and title of Her Majesty Queen Victoria to deal as she may think fit with the Zulu Chiefs and people, and with the Zulu country; and I agree and hereby sign by agreement, to accept from Sir Garnet Wolseley, G.C.M.G., K.C.B., as the representative of Her Majesty Queen Victoria, the Chieftainship of Zululand, &.c., subject to the following terms, conditions and limitations.

Those conditions included: each chief was to respect the

boundaries of the territory assigned to him through the Resident of the Division in which it was situated; the military system was to be renounced, and the men allowed to marry freely. Arms and ammunition were not to be imported in Zululand. Life was not to be taken without fair trial, and the practice of witchcraft would not be tolerated. Fugitives from justice were to be surrendered, and in all disputes the decision of the British Resident, Mr W.D. Wheelwright, was to be accepted. The document strongly echoed Frere's ultimatum.

Not all resistance had ended, however. In Mbilini's former stronghold near to the Tafelberg overlooking the Ntombe Drift, a force under Manyayoba kaMaqondo was still holding out. Lieutenant-Colonel B. Russell, 13th Hussars, led a force against the cavernous defences. Russell apparently attempted to smoke the defenders out, but in vain.

On Monday, 8th September, a week after the war had officially ceased, Colonel E.W. Bray of the 2nd Battalion, 4th (King's Own Royal) Regiment led a force comprising three companies of the 2nd/4th Foot, a detachment of Royal Engineers and party of irregular horse, against Manyayoba. A brief skirmish took place in which two non-commissioned officers of 2nd/4th fell, before the Engineers succeeded in blowing up the caves, thereby causing an end to any armed resistance. The British and Colonial Forces had sustained their last casualties and the war was finally over.

How many Zulu had perished in the war? William Gladstone, who would defeat Disraeli in the 1880 General Election, gives a hint in his Midlothian Speech of December 1879: 'In Africa we had the record of 10,000 Zulus slain for no other offence than their attempt to defend their hearths and homes, their wives and their children.'

THE MEMORIAL TO THE BRITISH AND COLONIAL CASUALTIES
OF THE ANGLO-ZULU WAR, PIETERMARITZBURG, NATAL

British and Colonial Casualties of the Minor Actions of the Anglo-Zulu War

Saturday, 18th January 1879
(Whilst advancing near the White Mfolozi River)
WOUNDED IN ACTION
Wood's Irregulars
Privates: Jack and Slanyola (extent of wounds unknown)

Monday, 20th January 1879
(During a reconnaissance on Zungwini Mountain)
WOUNDED IN ACTION
Frontier Light Horse
Trooper J. Berry, slightly wounded
Trooper J. Randall, slightly wounded

Friday, 24th January 1879
(Near to Hlobane Mountain)
WOUNDED IN ACTION
Burgher Force
Privates: Budenbeck and Jelleome (extent of wounds unknown)

Monday, 10th February 1879
(During a cattle raid on Hlobane)
WOUNDED IN ACTION
Burgher Force
Private H. Bridenbach (extent of wound unknown)

Saturday, 15th February 1879
(During an assault on the Tafelberg stronghold near the Ntombe River)
Wood's Irregulars/Local Loyal Natives
KILLED IN ACTION
Two natives
MISSING IN ACTION (presumed dead)
One native
WOUNDED IN ACTION
Three natives

Saturday, 15th February 1879
(During an assault on Tolaka Mountain, on the Luneberg to Derby Road)

WOUNDED IN ACTION
Fairlie's Native Police
Swazi Mlongene, dangerously wounded
Swazi Ynyadi, severely wounded
Swazi Wilderman, severely wounded
Swazi Luka, severely wounded
Unnamed Swazi, severely wounded
Unnamed Swazi, slightly wounded

Thursday, 20th February 1879–Friday, 21st February 1879
(Whilst conducting an assault on the stronghold at Eloya Mountain)
WOUNDED IN ACTION
Fairlie's Native Police
Swazi Esau, slightly wounded
Swazi Kushlan, slightly wounded

Sunday, 18th May 1879
(During a reconnaissance on the Tafelberg Stronghold near the Ntombe River)
KILLED IN ACTION
Kaffarian Rifles
Trooper L. Larsen

Thursday, 5th June 1879
(During the burning of kraals on the Eastern Bank of the uPoko River)

KILLED IN ACTION
17th (Duke of Cambridge's Own) Lancers
Lieutenant and Adjutant F.J.C. Frith

WOUNDED IN ACTION
Frontier Light Horse
Trooper A. Stirling, slightly wounded

Natal Light Horse
Corporal A. McKinnon, slightly wounded
Trooper W. Seamer, slightly wounded

LIEUTENANT AND
ADJUTANT F.J.C. FRITH,
17TH LANCERS

LIEUTENANT
J.H. SCOTT-DOUGLAS,
2ND/21ST FUSILIERS

Baker's Horse
Trooper D. O'Leary, severely wounded
Trooper S. Vogan, slightly wounded

Saturday, 7th June 1879
(Near the Ntombe River)
KILLED IN ACTION
Civilian
Acting Interpreter H. Filter

Border Police
Six natives (names unknown)

Monday, 30th June 1879
(Ambushed whilst on signalling duties near to kwaMagwaza Mission)
KILLED IN ACTION
2nd Battalion, 21st Royal Scots Fusiliers
Lieutenant J.H. Scott-Douglas

17th (Duke of Cambridge's Own) Lancers
Corporal W. Cotter

Monday, 8th September 1879
(During a skirmish with Manyayoba kaMaqondo's forces, the Tafelberg Stronghold)

KILLED IN ACTION
2nd Battalion, 4th (King's Own Royal) Regiment of Foot
Sergeant-Major E. Smith
Corporal I. Pomfret

Bibliography

Official Sources
Public Record Office, Kew
WO16 Series, Regimental and Corps Pay Lists
WO32/7706-84, WO33/33, Zulu War Correspondence
WO146/1, Submissions for the DCM
(All the above items are Crown Copyright, 1990)
Parliamentary Papers (Blue Books) 1879, 1880
War Office Army Lists, January–July 1879, July–December 1879

Newspapers and Journals
The Graphic 1878–1882
The Illustrated London News, 1879
The London Gazette, 1879, 1880, 1882
Punch, 1879
The Natal Mercury Supplement 21/1/1929
The Strand Magazine, 1891
Journal of the Society for Army Historical Research (various dates)
Soldiers of the Queen, The Journal of the Victorian Military Society
   (various dates)
Various Regimental Journals, including:
Men of Harlech, Diehard's Doings, The Diehards (various dates)

Private Papers
The collected papers of Lady C. Frere covering 1874–1882

Published Books
Abbot, P.E., *Recipients of the Distinguished Conduct Medal, 1855
   –1909*, Essex 1987
Adams, J., *The South Wales Borderers*, London 1968
Ashe, W. & Wyatt-Edgell, E.V., *The Story of the Zulu Campaign*,
   London 1880
Atkinson, C.T., *The South Wales Borderers, 24th Foot 1689–1937*,
   Cambridge 1937
Bancroft, J.W., *Rorke's Drift*, Tunbridge Wells 1988

Barlee, E. (comp), *Life of the Prince Imperial of France*, London 1880

Barthorp, M., *The Zulu War: A Pictorial History*, Poole 1980

Bennett, I., *Eyewitness in Zululand*, London 1989

Binns, C.T., *The Last Zulu King – The Life and Death of Cetshwayo*, London 1963

Buchan, J., *History of the Royal Scots Fusiliers, 1678–1918*, London 1925

Butler, W.F., *Sir William Butler, An Autobiography*, London 1913

Child, D. (Ed.), *The Zulu War Journal of Colonel Henry Harford, C.B.*, Pietermaritzburg 1978

Clammer, D., *The Zulu War*, London 1973

Clements, W.H., *The Glamour and Tragedy of the Zulu War*, London 1936

Coghill, P., *Whom the Gods Love*, Halesowen, 1968

Colenso, F.E., *The Ruin of Zululand*, London 1884

Colenso, F.E. and Durnford, E.C.L., *The History of the Zulu War and its Origin*, London 1880

Coupland, R., *Zulu Battle Piece – Isandhlwana*, London 1948

Currey, R.N., *Vinnicombe's Trek. A Family Chronicle of the time of the Zulu and Boer Wars*, London 1989

D'Arcy, P., *What Happened to a V.C.*, Dundalk 1973

Dumminy, A. and Ballard, C. (Eds.), *The Anglo-Zulu War: New Perspectives*, Pietermaritzburg 1981

Durnford, E., *A Soldier's Life and Work in South Africa 1872 to 1879. A Memoir of the Late Colonel A.W. Durnford, Royal Engineers*, London 1882

Egerton, R., *Like Lions They Fought*, London 1988

Elliot, W.J., *The Victoria Cross in Zululand and South Africa and How it was Won*, London 1882

Emery, F., *The Red Soldier, Letters from the Zulu War, 1879*, London 1977

Everett, H., *The History of the Somerset Light Infantry, 1685–1914*, London 1925

Featherstone, D., *Captain Carey's Blunder, The Death of the Prince Imperial*, London 1973

Fenn, T.E., *How I Volunteered For The Cape and What I Did There*, London 1879

French, G., *Lord Chelmsford and the Zulu War*, London 1939

Furneaux, R., *The Zulu War: Isandhlwana and Rorke's Drift*, London 1963

Glover, M., *Rorke's Drift – A Victorian Epic*, London 1975

Gon, P., *The Road to Isandlwana*, Johannesburg 1979

Grant, J., *British Battles on Land and Sea*, London 1894

Guy, J., *The Destruction of the Zulu Kingdom*, London 1979

Haggard, H. Rider, *Cetywayo and His White Neighbours*, London 1912

Hart, H.G., *Army Lists, 1878–80*

Hattersley, A.F. (Ed.), *Later Annals of Natal*, London 1938

Hicks Beach, V., *Life of Sir Michael Hicks Beach* (Vol. 1), London 1932

Holme, N., *The Silver Wreath – Being the 24th Regiment at Isandhlwana and Rorke's Drift*, 1879, London 1979

Holt, H.P., *The Mounted Police of Natal*, London 1913

Jones, L.T. (Ed.), *Reminiscences of the Zulu War* by John Maxwell, Cape Town 1979

Knight, I.J. (Ed.), *There will be an Awful Row at Home About This* (Revised), Shoreham-by-Sea 1987

Laband, J., *Fight us in the Open*, Pietermaritzburg 1985

Laband, J., *The Battle of Ulundi*, Pietermaritzburg 1985

Laband, J.P.C. and Thompson, P.S., *Field Guide to the War in Zululand and the Defence of Natal 1879* (2nd Edition with minor revisions), Pietermaritzburg 1987

Laband, J.P.C. and Thompson, P.S., *War Comes to Umvoti: The Natal Zululand Border*, Durban 1980

Laband, J.P.C. and Thompson, P.S., *The Buffalo Border*, Pietermaritzburg 1983

Laband, J. and Wright, J., *King Cetshwayo KaMpande*, Pietermaritzburg 1980

Lloyd, A., *The Zulu War*, London 1973

Lucas, T.J., *The Zulus and the British Frontiers*, London 1879

Lugg, H.C., *Historic Natal and Zululand*, Pietermaritzburg 1949

Lummis, W.M., *Padre George Smith of Rorke's Drift*, Norwich 1978

MacKinnon, J.P. and Shadbolt, S., *The South African Campaign*, London 1880

Marter, R.J.C., *The Capture of Cetywayo, King of the Zulus*, London 1880

McToy, E.D., *A Brief History of the 13th Regiment (P.A.L.I.) in*

South Africa During the Transvaal and Zulu Difficulties, 1877–8–9, Devonport 1880

Molyneaux, W.C.F., *Campaigning in South Africa and Egypt*, London 1896

Moodie, D.C.F., *The History of the Battles and Adventures of the British, the Boers and the Zulus in Southern Africa*, Adelaide 1879

Morris, D.R., *The Washing of the Spears*, London 1966

Mossop, G., *Running the Gauntlet*, London 1937

Norbury, H.F., *The Naval Brigade in South Africa During the Years 1877–78–79*, London 1880

Norris-Newman, C.L., *In Zululand with the British Throughout the War of 1879*, London 1880 (Reprinted 1988)

Parr, H.H., *A Sketch of the Kafir and Zulu Wars*, London 1880

Parry, D.H., *The Death or Glory Boys – The Story of the 17th Lancers*, London 1899

Paton, G., Glennie, F. and Penn Symons, W., *Historical Records of the 24th Regiment*, Devonport 1892

Pimblett, W., *In Africa with the Union Jack*, London (N.D.) Circa 1886

Porter, R. daC., *Warfare against uncivilised races; or how to fight greatly superior forces of an uncivilised and badly-armed enemy*, Royal Engineers Professional Papers, Prize Essay for 1881, London 1882

Smith-Dorrien, H., *Memories of Forty-Eight Years Service*, London 1925

Stalker, J. (Ed.), *The Natal Carbineers*, Pietermaritzburg and Durban 1912

Streatfeild, F.N., *Reminiscences of an Old 'Un*, London 1911

Tomasson, W.H., *With the Irregulars in the Transvaal and Zululand*, London 1881

Vijn, C. (Trans. and Ed. J.W. Colenso), *Cetshwayo's Dutchman*, London 1880 (reprinted 1988)

War Office, Rothwell, J.S. (compiler), *Narrative of Field Operations Connected with the Zulu War of 1879*, London 1881 (reprinted 1907 and 1989)

Webb, C. de B. and Wright, J.B., *A Zulu King Speaks: Statements made by Cetshwayo kaMpande on the history and customs of his people*, Pietermaritzburg and Durban 1978

Whitton, F.E., *Deeds Which Should Not Pass Away*, Edinburgh 1939

Wilmot, A., *History of the Zulu War*, London 1880

Wood, (H.)E., *From Midshipman to Field Marshal*, Vol. II, London 1906

Wood, (H.)E., *Winnowed Memories*, London 1918

Wood, (H.)E., *British Battles on Land and Sea*, London 1914

Index

A complete index of the casualties of the Anglo–Zulu War would in itself be a lengthy volume. Persons wishing to research a particular casualty will find them listed in the action in which they were killed or wounded.